Cataloging Music

A Manual for Use With AACR 2

by

Richard P. Smiraglia

Second Edition

Soldier Creek Press

Lake Crystal, Minnesota

1986

Library of Congress Cataloging-in-Publication Data

```
Smiraglia, Richard P., 1952-
   Cataloging music.

   Bibliography: p.
   Includes index.
   1. Cataloging of music -- Handbooks, manuals, etc.
2. Cataloging of sound recordings -- Handbooks, manuals,
etc.  3. Anglo-American cataloguing rules.  I. Swanson,
Edward, 1941-   .  II. Title.
ML111.S63  1986      025.3'488          86-31615
ISBN 0-936996-19-6
```

Edited by Edward Swanson

Artwork by David Kaun

Cover photo by T. Kilton

Typesetting by Sharon Olson and Nancy Loewen
Layout by Sharon Olson

Computer expertise provided by Tim Olson

This edition was produced using an Apple Macintosh Plus computer; Thunderware ThunderScan installed in
an Apple Imagewriter printer; Microsoft Word 1.05 program; Apple MacPaint program; Aldus Pagemaker
program; Apple LaserWriter printer.

Soldier Creek Press
Lake Crystal, Minnesota 56055

To *Marcia Jane* and *Marilyn Jean*
who made this edition possible

CONTENTS

ILLUSTRATIONS

PREFACE

The first edition of this book grew from a set of eighteen cataloging examples used in a music librarianship practicum and was expanded from a workshop outline used in continuing education programs that began with the implementation of the second edition of the *Anglo-American Cataloguing Rules (AACR 2)* in 1980-81. It incorporated Library of Congress published policy statements because of the need for a single source of *basic* information on how to apply *AACR 2* to music materials.

This second edition updates the original text and covers areas I neglected in the first edition, most of which were brought to my attention by readers or students. I hope that the combination of Library of Congress policy and my advice will continue to provide useful guidance to those who must often deal with music materials without benefit of vast musical expertise.

A secondary goal of this book is to serve as a handbook for the beginning music cataloger. The experienced professional music librarian will find little new or different in this volume, although, as stated above, another of its goals is to provide a single collection of the pertinent policy decisions.

I have not undertaken to explain either the basic principles of cataloging or the basic tenets of music librarianship. Although both apply to music cataloging, both are better dealt with elsewhere. This manual does presuppose a thorough understanding of *AACR 2* as revised, as well as a familiarity with certain basic source material for cataloging, such as *Cataloging Service Bulletin*.

The introduction addresses revisions to *AACR 2* since its publication in 1978 and major issues still under discussion. The first four chapters are the narrative. In Chapter 1 the various rules from *AACR 2* chapters 5 (Music) and 6 (Sound recordings) are treated together to better illustrate both the similarities in the approach to cataloging and the differences in the types of data in the various areas of the description. Chapters 2-4 deal with access points, particularly uniform titles, perhaps the most confusing aspect of both music cataloging and *AACR 2*. Throughout, the numbers of the rules under discussion are given in boldface.

The approach implicit in *AACR 2*, where the first step is to create a description of the item in hand and the second step is to provide access to the works contained therein, is also recommended here. The item-specific vs. work-specific distinction is repeatedly critical in music cataloging, and the reader will no doubt become increasingly aware of this while working through the text.

Chapter 5 offers a variety of cataloging examples that can be used as exercises or simply for the cataloger's reference. While none of the examples is particularly complex, taken together they constitute a fairly comprehensive selection and are not at all atypical of the types of music materials found in many libraries of whatever variety.

Chapter 6 is a compilation of the most basic of music reference tools. These are tools that I have found in many general library collections, and it is my intention to draw attention to their usefulness in both identifying basic musical terminology and in a beginning approach to authority work. Professional music librarians will quickly recognize the limitations of this list, although each of the sources named is reasonably reliable.

Another good source of music cataloging tools is the list of "Reference Works in the Music Section" that appears occasionally in *Music Cataloging Bulletin* and its index/supplements. For the ambitious neophyte I strongly recommend a good course in music bibliography, which can be taken in most graduate schools of music and in many schools of librarianship as well. Chapter 6 also includes complete bibliographic details of the thematic catalogs authorized by the Library of Congresss for use in formulating uniform titles.

The concordance of rule interpretations and music cataloging decisions has been updated and incorporated with an index to rule numbers used in this text. Finally, a glossary of terms peculiar to music cataloging that are not defined in *AACR 2* and an index have been added at the request of many readers of the first edition.

Once again I feel constrained to point to the current state of unrest vis-à-vis the rules for cataloging music materials using *AACR 2*. Many rules have been revised since its publication. Most of these revisions have provided clarity and additional examples for what had been vague rules. Major revisions (such as the reorganization of the rules for music uniform titles) are still in the works as I write this new edition. These revisions can be expected to appear in the upcoming consolidated reprinting of *AACR 2* (now scheduled for 1988). This manual, like its predecessor, is based on the rules as they currently are applied by the Library of Congress.

Urbana, Illinois
August 16, 1986

ACKNOWLEDGMENTS

I wish to thank all those who have contributed to the shaping of this book. First, I owe a great deal to Arlene G. Taylor (School of Library Service, Columbia University) and Sheila S. Intner (Graduate School of Library & Information Science, Simmons College), whose advice and encouragement have kept me fortified through the writing of both editions. Dean P. Jensen (Library, Vandercook College of Music) was my graduate assistant in 1984-85; it is due to his untiring assistance that the rule interpretations and cataloging decisions issued between the two editions of this book were compiled, concorded, and inserted in the text. Mary Joan Edwards, my devoted secretary, spent many long hours at the microcomputer converting the typed first edition into the machine-readable second edition. Richard H. Hunter (Music Section, Special Materials Cataloging Division, Library of Congress) and Joan Swanekamp (Sibley Music Library, Eastman School of Music) read the first edition for me and have contributed much to this edition as well, as has David Sommerfield (Music Section, Special Materials Cataloging Division, Library of Congress). Ben Tucker (Office for Descriptive Cataloging Policy, Library of Congress) has contributed with his patience and willingness to shape changes in Library of Congress policies pertaining to music in the popular idiom so that they could appear in this edition. Likewise, Michael Gorman (University of Illinois at Urbana-Champaign Library), editor of *AACR 2*, has shown me advance copy of rules undergoing change, so that my text might correspond to the new rules when they are issued. Finally, my special thanks to my publisher, Nancy B. Olson, and my editor, Edward Swanson, for their advice, but mostly for their patience.

INTRODUCTION

This is a book about descriptive cataloging (some would say author and title cataloging) of printed music and musical sound recordings. Cataloging music materials for any library can be a challenge. Chief sources of information can be deceptive in appearance ("list" title pages on printed music, or sound recording labels, for example), and sometimes the information they provide is insufficient for one to be able to establish an intelligible entry. Establishing access points can be complicated and confusing for those who are not well grounded in music bibliography. No matter how detailed the rules in the *Anglo-American Cataloguing Rules,* second edition (*AACR 2*), special knowledge or special techniques may be required to construct a "correct" bibliographic record for a musical item.

Nevertheless, cataloging is, after all, cataloging. The music cataloger begins by creating a transcription of title, statement of responsibility, and details of publication from integral sources of information. A physical description is formulated, and notes are made where needed to further clarify the content of the item. Once the description is completed, access points are formulated to serve as index entries in the catalog. For music materials, access points are made under headings for composers (usually in conjunction with a uniform title) and performers, as well as under the usual headings for editors, compilers, titles, and series.

AACR 2 provides an integrated approach to descriptive cataloging of all types of materials. General rules appear in chapter 1 and in chapters 21-26, which apply to all kinds of materials cataloged by libraries. Special rules for music materials appear in chapters 5 (Music) and 6 (Sound recordings), and in special sections of chapters 21 (Choice of access points) and 25 (Uniform titles). The music cataloger must be familiar with the general rules as well as the special rules for music.

Cataloging practice in the United States is heavily influenced by the policies of the Library of Congress. Rule Interpretations (RIs) are isssued by the Office for Descriptive Cataloging Policy and provide clarification of many rules as well as examples of their application. Music Cataloging Decisions (MCDs) are issued by the Music Section, Special Materials Cataloging Division, and further elucidate specific provisions of the rules as they apply to music cataloging.

Finally, any cataloger of special materials must be familiar with the literature and bibliography of that body of material, and music is no exception. Specialized reference sources must be consulted during the cataloging process to determine how best to relate a particular description to the catalog in general and to the entire body of music literature in particular. This book is one attempt to bring together in one place information about and instruction in the use of all three of these aspects.

Cataloging is a dynamic profession, changing by adopting new techniques as new information and new technologies become available to the profession. The remainder of this introduction focuses on the current status of *AACR 2*, Library of Congress policies, and some particularly difficult issues in music cataloging.

AACR 2, 1986

When *AACR 2* appeared in 1978 there were many lacunae in the rules devoted to cataloging music materials. In some instances rules were too vague, referring the cataloger to book-oriented instructions in general chapters. Some music-specific rules contained insufficient detail to produce useful bibliographic records with the degree of interlibrary consistency that has come to be expected in the era of online bibliographic networks. Some rules were controversial because they produced results that were unpopular with music librarians and, in a few cases, with the public who had grown accustomed to the practices of earlier cataloging codes. Some provisions were missing entirely.

The intervening years have provided music catalogers the opportunity to fine-tune the rules in *AACR 2*. Some provisions of the *ISBD(PM): International Standard Bibliographic Description for Printed Music*, which was unfinished at the time *AACR 2* was being compiled, have been adopted. The five year review of the *ISBD(NBM): International Standard Bibliographic Description for Nonbook Materials*, which included provisions for sound recordings, led to much discussion which has influenced the rule revision process. Due in large part to the efforts of the Music Library Association and the Canadian Association of Music Libraries, national cataloging committees in the United States and

Canada have been influenced to put forth proposals for revision of *AACR 2*, most of which have been accepted by the Joint Steering Committee for Revision of the Anglo-American Cataloguing Rules (JSC).

Since 1978, three sets of revisions to *AACR 2* have been published. Revisions of consequence for music cataloging include the following:

1.1E5	
1.1F4	} Parallelisms
5.1D1	
1.1G2, 6.1G2	Unit description
1.4F5	Phonogram copyright
1.4F6	Pressing date
1.5B4	Duration as extent of item
5.1B1	Transcription of music title proper
5.3	Musical presentation statement
5.5B1	Extent of item for printed music
5.7B19	Plate and publisher's numbers
21.23C-D	Choice of entry for sound recordings
25.2A	Expanded use of uniform titles
25.29H3	*Songs* in the popular idiom
25.32	Parts of a musical work

Several other rules have been revised for essentially editorial reasons.

Probably the most significant revisions have been:

1) The introduction of area 3, Musical presentation statement, for printed music. This area of *AACR 2*, defined as "Material specific details," was formerly reserved for use with cartographic materials and serial publications. This provision, introduced in the *ISBD(PM)*, provides for the transcription of words or phrases on the chief source of a music publication that identify the physical format of the music (e.g., score, parts, etc.)

2) Revision of rule 1.4F5 to allow transcription of phonogram copyright dates with the symbol "p." This symbol was introduced in the early 1970s when copyright protection was extended to sound recordings. Formerly *AACR 2* allowed the transcription of copyright dates, but required the use of the symbol "c" as an indication of the fact of copyright. This was considered misleading by music librarians, because "c" dates that appear on sound recordings indicate copyright of the artwork or accompanying text, but may have little or no relation to the date of release of the recorded performance.

3) The revision of rule 21.23C-D, Choice of entry for sound recordings, to prevent misleading entry under principal performer of a sound recording anthology of western art music lacking a collective title. These entries, permissible under the rules as first published, seemed to indicate that the performer chosen as main entry had composed the first work whose title was transcribed in area 1 of the description. The revised rule allows such entries for music in the popular idiom, where the titles of the works are commonly identified with the name of the performer, and restricts its use for western art music, which is entered under the heading appropriate to the first work.

One revision that has not been attempted is the revision of rule 25.27A, the rule for choosing the basis of the uniform title for a musical work. There has been much dissatisfaction with this rule, because it requires works to be entered under the original title. For Russian composers in particular, this means that uniform titles are now formulated from romanized Russian-language titles, which many consider to be unrecognizable (even indecipherable) to English-speaking library users. Despite the dissatisfaction with this provision, no consensus has been reached in the music library community on a better approach.

This book addresses the provisions of *AACR 2* as it stands today, including the three sets of revisions. Proposed revisions still being considered by the JSC are discussed below.

LIBRARY OF CONGRESS POLICIES

As mentioned earlier, there are at present many RIs and MCDs from the Library of Congress that serve to modify, explicate, and/or alter the effect of the provisions in *AACR 2* as published. All of these statememts that are pertinent for music cataloging are printed in this book. As this edition goes to press there are over eighty such statements. There are today fewer RIs than there were at the time of the writing of the first edition of this book. Many

RIs provided detailed guidance where *AACR 2* formerly was vague on particular points. Some of these have been incorporated into the rule revisions listed above. This is probably the reason there are fewer RIs now than there were when the Library of Congress first implemented the code.

However, there are more MCDs now than before. Some provide guidance for catalogers at the Library of Congress and will be of use to other catalogers to the extent that they clarify changes in MARC records for music materials (which did not exist at the time the first edition of this book was published). Others seem to limit the effects of certain rules, such as the MCD for rule 6.0B1 that declares certain types of collective titles proper *not* collective titles proper. No doubt the Music Section will continue to provide MCDs as the rules continue to evolve.

MAJOR ISSUES

A "consolidated reprinting" of *AACR 2* is underway as this book goes to press. This reprinting will incorporate not only the revisions that have been issued to date, but also several rule revisions that have been approved or are still being discussed.

COMPACT DIGITAL AUDIO DISCS

This new technology has taken the recording industry by storm. Many libraries that formerly collected standard 33 1/3 rpm discs have switched almost entirely to the new laser-read compact digital audio discs. *AACR 2* was reviewed for rules that would require revision to accomodate this new technology, and many rules were revised during 1985. These revisions will be incorporated in the "consolidated reprinting" of *AACR 2*. However, the provisions were published in *Cataloging Service Bulletin* numbers 28 and 30 and are already being applied by the Library of Congress. Because they now constitute "LC practice," their use is required by most online bibliographic networks. These provisions are described in this book, and the cataloging examples have been revised accordingly.

ORDER OF RULES FOR UNIFORM TITLES

Many music catalogers found the rules for construction of uniform titles difficult to apply at the time *AACR 2* was first published. When the consolidated reprinting was agreed upon by the publishing bodies, the JSC encouraged music catalogers to submit a proposal for editorial changes that would place these rules in the order in which they are to be applied. A key provision of this proposal was the introduction of the term "initial title element." An initial title element is the base title on which the cataloger builds to create a unique access point for a work. When the consolidated reprinting of *AACR 2* appears the rules for music uniform titles in chapter 25 will be in the new order, and it is hoped they will be easier to apply. There are, however, no substantive changes in these rules.

MUSIC IN THE POPULAR IDIOM

The various committees involved in the revision of *AACR 2* have heard a great deal in the past two years about "music in the popular idiom." Some catalogers have thought that *AACR 2* had an inherent bias toward Western art music (what is often referred to as "classical" music) and that certain provisions should be modified to allow for catalog entries that make sense not only to catalogers but to users of music collections as well.

One notable example is the revision of rule 25.29H3. This rule instructs the cataloger on the addition of terms indicating the medium of accompaniment for works whose titles are "Songs," "Lieder," or some other foreign language equivalent. The rule was initially devised as a shortcut for catalogers of traditional songs, for which the medium of performance is almost always voice and piano. If accompaniment was for other than piano, it was to be indicated; otherwise, no indication of accompanying medium was to be supplied because the user of the catalog could be expected to infer the medium of performance from the title "Songs." This provision was not to be applied to collective uniform titles constructed according to rule 25.36B.

Some catalogers believed that other, less well-informed, catalogers would apply these provisions to popular songs. This was highly unlikely, because the provision was specifically limited to works whose *titles* were "Songs," "Lieder," etc. (admittedly an unlikely occurrence for a "popular" song). Nevertheless, the rule was revised to incorporate the instruction that it should not be applied to popular music, for which accompaniment is usually unspecified, but usually includes a guitar. (Perhaps the more realistic approach would have been to remove the example at rule 25.29H3 that illustrated guitar accompaniment.)

Because rule revision is a relatively conservative process, and because those involved prefer to deal with whole issues rather than taking a piecemeal approach to rule revision, music experts were asked to investigate *AACR 2* to identify all rules that applied to works realized through performance and, in particular, musical works commonly referred to as "popular." It quickly became apparent to the various committees that nonmusicians were confused about the term "popular music." Most people thought that it meant music that was very popular.

However, in music the term has a specific meaning, and consequently the phrase "music in the popular idiom" was introduced. This phrase was devised as a signal to catalogers that a particular style of composition and performance was under discussion, rather than music that is merely well loved. It is difficult to pin down sufficient details about this style of music so as to introduce into the cataloging rules simple terminology that would be understandable to *all* catalogers, not just music specialists.

Many hours have been spent in attempts to revise rule 25.31B2, the provisions of which allow the addition of the abbreviation "arr ." to indicate that a work has been rewritten for a medium of performance not intended by the original composer. Readers should be aware of the one incontrovertible fact about music in the popular idiom: it is not written at all. It is usually a melody that is played or sung (i.e., performed). It may then be written down (i.e., transcribed) with chord symbols that indicate the general direction accompaniment, if any, should take. Because the music never existed in a specific written version that was intended to be realized in a manner as close as possible to a composer's original intention, it is not possible for it to exist in an "arranged" (i.e., altered) version.

There are several implications. First, printed music in the popular idiom is almost always a transcription of a performance. Most Western art music, on the other hand, is written first, then performed. Second, performers of music in the popular idiom traditionally improvise a great deal when they perform. This means that no two performances will be identical, because improvisation is an innately human activity and is as dependent on the performer's mood as on his or her musical talent. (The problem for rule revision is that these things can also be true of performances of Western art music. Further, some performers of music in the popular idiom do not improvise!)

Finally, as noted before, it is almost impossible to pin down the transient nature of this music in terminology that is universally understandable and that does not do injustice to non-Western art music. As a consequence, revision of rules pertinent to works realized through performance is not only difficult, but may be impossible. This book introduces these concepts and provides instructions where appropriate.

CHAPTER 1: DESCRIPTION

CHOOSING THE CHIEF SOURCE OF INFORMATION

The first task, and therefore the first problem, in the preparation of catalog records for music and sound recordings is determining the source of the information that describes the item. In cataloging books the cataloger usually has a title page to use as the chief source of information. Some music materials do have title pages, but others do not, and therefore the cataloger must use a title page substitute. Sound recordings, by virtue of their physical format, do not have title pages.

SCORES

5.0B1, 2.0B1 Printed music is often issued without a title page. In other cases the title page will consist of a list of titles and other title information (a "list" title page), frequently with the title of the particular publication underlined (see Figure 1a).

Of course, when a monograph-style title page is present it is used as the chief source of information. When there is no typical title page, but a "list" title page is present, the cataloger should choose whichever of the "list" title page, cover, or caption provides the fullest information. In Figures 1b and 1c, the caption is chosen because the cover has no information about the work and because it gives a fuller description of the work than the "list" title page.

When there is no "list" title page, the cataloger should choose a title page substitute according to the instructions in rule 2.0B1. The part chosen as substitute must be the part that supplies the most complete information. Possible substitutes are the cover, half-title page, caption, colophon, running title, etc. The part used as title page substitute must then be identified in a note.

If the prescribed source of information is the chief source of information, but the information is not available from the chief source, take it from one of the following sources (in this order of preference): caption, cover, colophon, other preliminaries, other sources.

Bear in mind that printed music has a long tradition of decorative title pages. To be a cover, it must be printed on material (usually heavier paper or card stock) that is different from the material on which the music is printed. A colorful title page is not necessarily a cover. In Figure 2 the title page looks like a cover, but it really is not.

MUSIC FOR OBOE

Edited & Arranged by Evelyn Rothwell

Arne, M.	Pastorale
Bach, J. S.	Adagio
Besozzi, A.	Sonata
Boyce, W.	Gavotte & Gigue
Couperin, F.	Le Bavolet Flottant
Dandrieu, J. F.	Les Fifres
Field, J.	Nocturne
Handel, G.	Air & Rondo
Loeillet, J. B.	Sonata in C major
Marcello, B.	Largo & Allegretto
Mozart, W. A.	Oboe Quartet
Rameau, J. P.	Les Tendres Plaintes
Sammartini, G.	Sonata in G
Tchaikowsky, P.	The Canary

N.B.   See separate list for other works for Oboe.

NORSK MUSIKFORLAG A/S
OSLO

A.B. NORDISKA MUSIKFORLAGET
STOCKHOLM

J & W. CHESTER LTD · LONDON
Made in Great Britain

WILHELM HANSEN, MUSIK-FORLAG
COPENHAGEN

WILHELMIANA MUSIKVERLAG
FRANKFURT a. M.

Figure 1ₐ - List Title Page

WIND MUSIC

oboe and piano
Loeillet - Sonata in C major

J. & W. Chester Ltd.

Figure 1_b - Cover

Figure 1_c - Caption

3

Figure 2 - Decorative Title Page

SOUND RECORDINGS

6.0B1 For sound recordings the chief source of information is generally the label or labels as specified in rule 6.0B1. The single exception is made for collections, in which the accompanying textual matter of the container is preferred if it provides a collective title and the label or labels do not. In Figure 3 the labels do not provide a collective title. Because the container does, it is preferred as the chief source of information. Again, this substitute must be identified in a note. (See also MCD 6.0B1 under *Collective titles* below.)

TITLE AND STATEMENT OF RESPONSIBILITY AREA

TITLE PROPER

5.1B The initial step in the transcription of the title information requires that the cataloger make a judgment about the nature of the title itself. For example, if the title is "generic" (i.e., if it consists primarily of the name(s) of one or more types of composition), statements of other identifying elements such as medium of performance, opus number, etc., should be transcribed as part of the title proper.

    The reason for this exception is to prevent confusion in title indexes in which only the title proper is displayed. Without the identifying elements many titles would be indistinguishable. Consider, for example, two symphonies by Johannes Brahms. The titles in full are *Symphony 1, C minor, op. 68*, and *Symphony 4, E minor, opus 98*. If the identifying elements are not included in the title proper, each title would display as *Symphony*. To prevent this problem, such statements are transcribed as part of the title proper when the title consists of the name(s) of one or more types of composition.

Figure 3 - Collective Title Appears on Container

To make this determination the cataloger should first consider the title as a whole, then strip away all statements of medium of performance, enumeration, key, and/or date of composition. If what remains consists of the name of a type of composition, the title can be considered "generic." The following are "generic" titles (the essential element is in bold type);

> **Symphony** no. 3, A major, op. 56
> String **quintet**, no. 1, A major, opus 18
> Zwei **Praeludien und Fugen** für Orgel, op. posth. 7

In case of doubt about whether the term is the name of a type of composition, the cataloger should consult the rules for uniform titles (25.26-25.27) and/or a dictionary of musical terminology (see bibliography in Chapter 6). If the term is not defined there, it is unlikely that it is the name of a type of composition.

Names of types of compositon that are modified adjectivally are considered "distinctive." This means, quite simply, that the title is considered sufficient to identify the work without the addition of other identifying elements. The following would be considered "distinctive" titles (again the essential element is in bold type):

> **Easter fresco** for soprano, flute, horn, harp, and piano
> **Sinfonia mazedonia** Nr. 4, für grosses Orchester
> **Little suite** for 5 cellos (1956)
> **Also sprach Zarathustra** op. 30

The instruction in rule 5.1B1 is to consider other identifying elements as part of the title proper when the title is generic and to consider such elements as other title information when the title is distinctive. The following are proper transcriptions of the preceding examples:

> Symphony, no. 3, A major, op. 56 [GMD]
> String quintet no. 1, A major, opus 18 [GMD]
> Zwei Praeludien und Fugen für Orgel, op. posth. 7 [GMD]
> Easter fresco [GMD] : for soprano, flute, horn, harp, and piano
> Sinfonia mazedonia [GMD] : Nr. 4, für grosses Orchester
> Little suite [GMD] : for 5 cellos (1956)
> Also sprach Zarathustra [GMD] : op. 30

SERIAL NUMBERS

5.1B1 RI   Transcribe as part of the title proper a serial number (whether it appears as arabic or roman numerals or spelled out) which appears in conjunction with the title but without the designation "no." or its equivalent, regardless of the nature of the title.

> Antiphony II : variations on a theme of Cavafy

not   Antiphony : II : variations on a theme of Cavafy

(*CSB* 26:10)

MCD   Apply the first paragraph of this rule to titles consisting of the names of two or more types of composition only when each of the types named constitutes a more or less distinct part of the work or item. (In such cases the names of types are usually connected by a conjunction or other linking word).

> Zwei Praeludien und Fugen für Orgel, op. posth. 7

> Sonatas and partitas for solo violin, BWV 1001-1006

Figure 4 - Parallel Other Title Information

When a title consists of two words each of which alone would be the name of a type of composition, but the combination of the two words produces a distinctive title (cf. RI 25.27B, first paragraph), apply the second paragraph of this rule.

```
Fantaisie-impromptu : in C sharp minor, op. 66

Humoresque-bagatelles : op. 11
```

Note, however, that "trio sonata" (cf. 25.27E) and "chorale prelude" are each the name of *one* type of composition. (*MCB* 16:9:3)

PARALLEL STATEMENTS

5.1B1/5.1D1   While *AACR 2* provides detailed instructions for treatment of parallel titles, other title information, and statements of responsibility, there are no specific instructions for treatment of parallels when the repetition is not complete, although new examples at rule 5.1D1 provide a hint. Such incomplete parallels occur frequently in music materials. Figure 4 illustrates the problem. While the generic term appears only once, the key appears in three languages. The following Library of Congress Rule Interpretation offers further solutions to these problems:

5.1B1 RI   *Multiple Parallel Data*
When succeeding statements of key, etc., are broken up in the source rather than grouped together by language, transcribe the statements so that all elements in one language are together. Treat the first group of elements in one language as part of the title proper and precede each one after the first by an equals sign. Thus,

Concerto
D-Dur/D Major/Ré Majeur

für Horn und Orchester
for Horn and Orchestra
pour Cor et Orchestre

would then be transcribed as:

```
    Concerto, D-Dur, für Horn und Orchester = D major, for horn and
orchestra = ré majeur, pour cor et orchestre
```

(Record all the parallel elements; do not apply the provisions for omission in 1.1D2.)

Adopt the following solutions for data that are other title information or statements of responsibility that are only partially repeated from language to language. For such a problem with a statement of responsibility, rule 1.1F11 provides a solution in the second paragraph ("If it is not practicable ...") by saying to give the statement that matches the language of the title proper and to omit the other statement(s).

... [Czech title proper]
Revidoval -- Revidiert von Antonín Myslík

```
    ... / revidoval Antonín Myslík.
```

There is no comparable "If it is not practicable ..." provision in the rule for other title information, yet the same difficulty of transcription arises with partial repetition of other title information. Nonetheless apply the same idea to other title information.

Sonata a velocità pazzesca
per   for
cembalo

The transcription would be:

```
Sonata a velocità pazzesca : per cembalo
```

If no real match in languages is possible, then give the first of the language forms, matching at least the other title information with the statement of responsibility if possible.

Chief source

Gregor Joseph Werner
Concerto per la camera a 4
für   for
Violoncello & Piano
Herausgegeben und bearbeitet von   Edited and arranged by
Richard Moder

Transcription

```
Concerto per la camera : a 4 : für Violoncello & Piano /
Gregor Joseph Werner; herausgegeben und bearbeitet von Richard
Moder
```

(*CSB* 26:10-11)

STATEMENTS OF RESPONSIBILITY

SCORES

5.1F/1.1F14   Rule 1.1F14 instructs the cataloger to transcribe statements of responsibility even though no person or body is named. Such statements appear frequently on music publications. It is easy to confuse such statements as "vocal score with piano," or "edition for 2 pianos" with edition statements, or musical presentation statements (see discussions of 5.2 and 5.3 below). Statements indicating an arrangement or version of the musical work are statements of responsibility because they imply the work of a person who has altered the musical content of the work for the publication.

```
My fair lady / music by Frederick Loewe ; book and lyrics by
Alan Jay Lerner ; vocal score ...

Symphonien / Beethoven ; Klavierauszug von Franz Liszt ...
```

POPULAR MUSIC FOLIOS

Popular music folios (sometimes referred to as "pop-folios") are usually transcriptions of recordings, sold as scores for voice and piano with guitar chord diagrams and chord symbols. These are primarily commercial products, but they can be used by an ensemble that wants to perform in the style of the popular music group represented. Because these often mirror popular sound recordings (record albums), their covers and/or title pages are often the same as the front of the container of the corresponding recording. This presents a problem because the featured name on the title page (hence the chief source of information) is usually that of the performer, which is rarely the name of the composer(s) of the music represented within. A new Library of Congress Rule Interpretation allows the names of such performing groups to be transcribed as statements of responsibility.

5.1F1 RI When the performer's name featured on the chief source of information on a popular music folio does not appear within the title proper, transcribe it as a statement of responsibility.

        40 hour week / Alabama

        Once upon a time / Donna Summer

(unpublished RI)

SOUND RECORDINGS

6.1F1. *AACR 2*'s use of the statement of responsibility area in chapter 6 presents special choices to the cataloger of sound recordings. The problem is what names to include in this area. The rule requires, of course, the transcription of names of composers of music, authors of texts, and collectors of field recordings. These names are transcribed because they identify the persons or bodies responsible for the material that has been recorded. This usage is consistent with the instructions for printed materials.

  Sound recordings also have performers, and rule 6.1F1 makes a distinction between performers of highly improvisational music, whose names are to be transcribed in the statement of responsibility area, and other performers, whose names are transcribed in a note. A Library of Congress Rule Interpretation adds this caveat:

6.1F1 RI The rule allows performers who do more than perform to be named in the statement of responsibility. Accept only the most obvious cases as qualifying for the statement of responsibility. (*CSB* 11:15)

  The point here is to recognize as a type of author those performers who play a creative role in the performance of music. In traditional Western "classical" music, the performer recreates a composer's musical idea (performance), adding nuance and perhaps ornamentation (interpretation). Other types of music, however, do not tend to be as strictly composed. In these cases the performer adds musical ideas to the preconceived sketch (for example, the jazz musician who improvises on a set of chord changes). In the latter case the name of the performer should be transcribed in the statement of responsibility.

SOUND RECORDINGS DESCRIBED AS A UNIT

6.1G Rule 6.1G1 gives the cataloger a choice when describing a sound recording that has no collective title. According to the rule, one may describe such a recording as a unit or one may make a separate description for each separately titled work on the recording. The Library of Congress now describes all sound recordings with unit descriptions whether the recording has a collective title or not. This means that separate bibliographic records for individual works, linked by "with notes," no longer appear among Library of Congress cataloging. This policy does create some problems for catalogers preparing unit descriptions.

COLLECTIVE TITLES

1.1B3 The cataloger should be aware that it is entirely possible for the name of a performer to be considered as a collective title. The decision in this instance will be based on the prominence, wording, and typography of the labels, container, and accompanying textual matter of the recorded collection. Generally, when the name of the

Figure 5 - Performer's Name As Title Proper

be a collective title. Figure 5 shows one such case.
The following Library of Congress Rule Interpretation applies:

1.1B3 RI   If the chief source shows the name of an author or the name of a performer before the titles of the individual works, and there is doubt whether the publisher, etc., intended the name to be a collective title proper or a statement of responsibility, treat the name as the title proper. Exception: If the works listed are musical compositions and the name is that of the composer of the works, treat the name as a statement of responsibility in cases of doubt.

If the chief source being followed is the label of a sound recording, and the decision is to treat the name as a title proper, but one name appears on the label of one side and another name on the second side, transcribe the two names as individual titles (separated by a period-space). (*MCB* 13:2:3-4)

However, according to the following Library of Congress Music Cataloging Decision, some types of collective titles are to be disregarded.

6.0B1 MCD   For sound recordings containing two works of the same type by one composer without a collective title on the label(s), do not consider as a collective title a title on the container or accompanying material that is made up of the name of the type plus one or more of the following identifying elements for the two works: serial number, opus number, thematic index number, key.

> *On container:*
>   Piano concertos no. 25, K. 503, no. 26, K. 537
> Do not transcribe as collective title

> *On container:*
>   Sonatas no. 4, op. 7, and no. 11, op.22
> Do not transcribe as collective title

> *On container:*
>   Symphonies nos. 88 and 104 (London)
> Do not transcribe as collective title

but:

> *On container:*
>   The violin concertos / Serge Prokofiev
> Transcribe as collective title

> *On container:*
>   Les deux sonates pour violoncelle et piano
> Transcribe as collective title

> *On container:*
>   Ballets / Igor Stravinsky
> *(Contains Apollo and Orpheus)*
> Transcribe as collective title

(*MCB* 17:2:2-3)

TRANSCRIBING PERFORMER STATEMENTS OF RESPONSIBILITY

Occasionally when one is describing as a unit a sound recording that has no collective title, placement of the performer's statement of responsibility can be confusing. The problem arises chiefly in the description of 45 rpm popular music recordings. Typically there will be two musical works, one on each side, each with a different composer, but both performed by the same artist. Since there is rarely a container supplying a collective title, the cataloger must use the two labels together as the chief source of information.

1.1G2 Instructions in chapter one of *AACR 2* direct the cataloger to record the individual titles, together with the statements of responsibility that apply to each, in the order in which they appear in the item. Figure 6 shows such a case and its transcription.

GENERAL MATERIAL DESIGNATION

Placement of the general material designation (GMD) can also be a problem in unit description. Actually, a simple hierarchy can be constructed:

1) If there is only one work, the GMD follows the title proper:

        Symphony no. 2 in D, opus 36 [sound recording] / Beethoven

2) If there is more than one work but only one statement of responsibility (i.e., all by the same composer) the GMD immediately precedes the statement of responsibility:

```
La mer ; Khamma ; Rhapsody for clarinet and orchestra [sound
recording] / Claude Debussy
```

3) If there are works by different persons, the GMD follows the last statement of responsibility:

```
A charm of lullabies : op. 41 / Benjamin Britten. Two sonnets :
op. 87 / Edmund Rubbra. Four Shakespeare songs / E.J. Moeran.
Mädchen-lieder ; Zwei Gesänge, op. 91 / Brahms [sound recording]
```

EDITION AREA

The glossary in *AACR 2* defines edition:

1. In the case of books and booklike materials, all those copies of an item produced from substantially the same type image, whether by direct contact or by photographic methods. 2. In the case of nonbook materials, all the copies of an item produced from one master copy and issued by a particular publishing agency or a group of such agencies. Provided the foregoing conditions are fulfilled, a change of identity by the distributing body or bodies does not constitute a change of edition. (*AACR 2* p. 565)

Because of widespread misuse of the word "edition" and its foreign equivalents in the music profession, there has long been confusion about what information should be included in the edition area for printed music and sound recordings. (There is little actual difficulty with sound recordings, because they rarely carry edition statements of any kind.) An "in case of doubt" clause in rule 1.2B3 is of little help, because a wide variety of statements including the word "edition" can appear on music materials.

This is the first area of the bibliographic record where the distinction between the item cataloged and the work contained therein becomes crucial. (This will also be of importance in formulating notes and is vital in the formulation of uniform titles.) The cataloger must remain aware of the difference between the aesthetic (the musical idea that constitutes the work) and the corporeal (the physical manifestation of that idea).

5.2B2 The edition area records data about the production history of a specific physical manifestation. A musical work can be presented in an infinite and bewildering array of altered states. That is, it can be *arranged* for any medium of performance, such as a symphonic work arranged for two pianos, an organ prelude arranged for concert band, a vocal work arranged for different voice ranges, a violin concerto arranged for flute and piano, etc. Because arrangements have undergone human intervention (that is, a person has rewritten the work), they actually constitute versions of the original work. The problem is that chief sources of information will often utilize the word "edition" where "version" or "arrangement" perhaps would be more appropriate. Statements such as "Edition for 2 pianos" or "Klavierausgabe" ("Piano edition") are descriptive of the work contained and thus are not edition statements and should not be transcribed in the edition area.

To further complicate matters, the word "edition" can be used in a statement of responsibility to indicate a form of subsidiary authorship. Statements such as "Busoni edition" are statements of responsibility and should not be transcribed in the edition area unless they are accompanied by information indicative of their relationship to a specific physical manifestation. Such statements usually refer to the process of recording elements of interpretation such as fingerings, bowings, pedal marks, phrasing, breath indications, etc., and can be considered statements of responsibility relating to all editions [i.e., versions].

Last, but not least, are statements such as "Wilhelm-Hansen edition," "Edition Breitkopf," or "Harmonia-Uitgave." Despite the use of the word "edition," such statements (which always include the name of the publisher or one of its subsidiaries, and usually are found in conjunction with a stock number) are referred to as "publisher's numbers" (see 5.7B19 below) and are not edition statements.

Just what, then, should be transcribed in the edition area? Quite simply, those statements that refer to the production history of the physical item, "all those copies of an item produced from substantially the same type image." (*AACR 2* p. 565) Such statements are those that are common in monographs, such as "2nd ed.," "New ed.," "Rev. ed.," etc. However, with the exception of scholarly publications, such statements are rare both on printed music and on sound recordings. A Library of Congress Rule Interpretation further clarifies this point:

5.2B1 RI Focusing on the concept of "edition" for music publications, note the following points: care must be taken to distinguish between edition statements of the book type, which are found in music publications, and the very common musical presentation statements that should not be taken as edition statements. A musical presentation statement is one that indicates the version, the arrangements, etc., of a work or the form in which a work is presented in the item (i.e., the music format). Unfortunately, these statements frequently include the word "edition." Even so, they should not be regarded as edition statements.

Musical presentation statements go in the statement of responsibility when the music itself is meant; a *version* of the music, an *arrangement* of the music, even a *transposition* of the music. In all these cases an "author" is responsible for a changing of the original work. In other cases, when the music format is meant (e.g., edition in score format, edition as a set of parts), then the musical presentation statement should be transcribed according to 5.3. (*CSB* 33:32)

VOICE RANGE FOR SONGS

The single exception is the Library of Congress' decision to include statements of voice range in the edition area in some cases. Those cases are spelled out in the following Music Cataloging Decision:

5.2B2 MCD When a song, song cycle, or set or collection of songs bears a statement designating the voice range (as distinguished from a statement of medium of performance) that is not grammatically linked to the title, other title information, etc., transcribe the statement as an edition statement, whether or not it includes the work "edition" or its equivalent.

```
        Lieder / Franz Schubert ; herausgegeben von Walther Durr.
    -- Hohe Stimme (Originallage) ...

        Schubert-Album. -- Neue, kritisch durchgesehene Ausg. / von
    L. Benda, Ausg. für hohe Stimme ...

        Roadways / words by John Masefield ; music by Edith Rose.
    -- High key in F ...
```

but

```
        Lieder : eine Auswahl für hohe Stimmlage und Klavier ...

        Drei Lieder für eine hohe Stimme mit Klavierbegleitung ...
```

(*MCB* 13:6:2)

(See also discussions of MUSICAL PRESENTATION STATEMENTS and PUBLISHERS STOCK NUMBERS below.)

MUSICAL PRESENTATION STATEMENTS

5.3 A musical presentation statement is a word or phrase that appears in the chief source of information that indicates the format of the printed music in the item. Such statements are common on music publications and are transcribed in area 3 of the bibliographic description. Care must be taken not to confuse musical presentation statements with either edition statements or statements of responsibility (see discussions above).

```
    Classical symphony : op. 25 / Prokofieff. -- Score. -- New
York : ...

    4 quartets for flute, violin, viola, and cello / Mozart ; [edited by]
Jean-Pierre Rampal. -- Parts. -- New York : ...
```

PUBLICATION, DISTRIBUTION, ETC., AREA

5.4 Information for this area is recorded according to the general provisions of *AACR 2* chapter 1. A few notable exceptions are discussed below.

SCORES

PUBLISHER'S ADDRESS

1.4C7 The Library of Congress applies the option in rule 1.4C7 for music scores, adding the address of the publisher, distributor, etc., if it is given in the item according to the following Rule Interpretation:

1.4C7 RI Give the address of a publisher, etc., following the name of the place of publication, etc., only for a monograph cataloged according to chapter 2 or chapter 5 that meets these three conditions:

    a)   it was issued by a U.S. publisher, distributor, etc., whose address is given in the item being cataloged;

    b)   it was issued in the current three years;

    c)   it does not bear an ISBN or ISSN.

Do not apply 1.4C7 if two or more publishers, distributors, etc., are being recorded in the publication, etc., area. *Exception*: If one of the entities is a U.S. distributor for a monograph published outside of the U.S., give the address of the U.S. distributor if the item meets these four conditions:

    a)   the U.S. distributor is the only entity being recorded with the distributor's place of publication;

    b)   the U.S. distributor's address is given in the item;

    c) the item was issued in the current three years;

    d) the item lacks an ISBN or ISSN.

Apply 1.4C7 also to items in which the name of the publisher, distributor, etc., is unknown and the name of the U.S. manufacturer is given in the publication, etc., area (1.4G1) if the monograph meets these three conditions:

    a)   the manufacturer's address is given in the item;

    b)   the item was issued in the current three years;

    c)   the item lacks an ISBN or ISSN.

When applying 1.4C7, routinely repeat the name of the city in the address. For street addresses, abbreviate such words as "street," "avenue," "place," etc., according to normal usage. Omit unnecessary elements from the address (e.g., the name of the building when the street address or post office box is given). Do not bracket any of the elements given in the address. (*CSB* 13:3)

DATES OF PUBLICATION, DISTRIBUTION, ETC.

COPYRIGHT DATES

5.4F/1.4F Remember that the prescribed source of information for this area includes the first page of music. Because music publishers rarely indicate dates of publication, catalogers of printed music make great use of copyright dates. These dates more often than not appear at the bottom of the first page of music. (This handy practice allows the publisher to reissue a title from time to time with new covers for boosting sales without making any alterations in the original printing surface.) Because the first page of music is a prescribed source in this area of the description, the copyright date need not be bracketed.

5.4F, 1.4F6 It will often happen that printed music will carry neither a date of publication nor of copyright. In these cases the cataloger must supply an approximate date of publication. Several hints follow.

HIDDEN DATES

A good idea is to check the first and last pages of music to see if a printing date is present. If so, it can be used in lieu of a date of publication (see Figure 6). Care must be exercised in this regard. Frequently the date of composition or of the completion of the manuscript will be inscribed at the end of a score. Occasionally items reproduced photographically from manuscripts will carry a date that indicates the date of the printing of the staff paper. Such dates can be regarded as "hints" to estimate dates of publication (that is, if the work was completed in 1973 we know it could not have been published before then), but should not be transcribed as dates of publication.

East European publications often carry a colophon that might supply a date of publication. Also, East German publications will indicate a "Lizenz Nummer." As a rule of thumb, the final digits of the "Lizenz Nummer" will indicate the year of publication (see Figure 7).

POPULAR MUSIC FOLIOS

These collections usually are reprinted from a variety of individual sheet music publications. Copyright dates may appear at the foot of the first page of each song. Comparing the various copyright dates will give a hint as to the approximate date of publication of the collection, although care should be exercised that the information given in the bibliographic record is accurate. For example, if the span of copyright dates runs from 1974 to 1985, and the item is being cataloged in 1986, it is probable that the folio was published in 1986. Unfortunately, it is only probable; it could have been published in 1985.

Figure 6 - Printing Date

Lizenz-Nr. 472-155'332/57
Gesamtherstellung:
VEB Messe- und Musikaliendruck, Leipzig III/18/157

Figure 7 - Lizenz Nummer

There are at least three ways to express the probable date of publication in a case such as this. First, if it really seems probable that 1986 represents the year of publication it may be expressed as a questioned date:

        [1986?]

If there is any doubt on the cataloger's part about the reliability of the more specific estimate (for example, if the item were being cataloged early in 1986 it would seem more likely that it had been published in 1985) it may be expressed as follows:

        [1985 or 1986]

Finally, if the span between the last copyright date in the collection and the date the item is cataloged is greater than one year (for example, if the item above were to be cataloged in 1987) the date may be expressed as:

        [between 1985 and 1987]

PUBLISHER'S CATALOGS, NATIONAL BIBLIOGRAPHIES, ETC.

It is also possible to determine approximate dates of publication by consulting publisher's catalogs and/or published bibliographies. Such efforts, however, require a great deal of time and bibliographic skill. For most library catalogs the results do not justify the effort.

EARLY PRINTED MUSIC

For advice on the use of plate numbers, publisher's addresses, etc., in dating early printed music, see *Guide for Dating Early Published Music*, compiled by D.W. Krummel.

SOUND RECORDINGS

PLACE OF PUBLICATION

6.4 The presentation of standard bibliographic data in this area for sound recordings is an innovation in AACR 2. While such data are usually of less importance to users of sound recordings, they do help unify and integrate bibliographic records for all types of materials.

6.4C The cataloger should remember that although sound recordings might not present information in the same manner as other types of materials, the objective here is the same, namely to transcribe the information from the item itself. Information to be transcribed in this area may be taken from the labels, the accompanying textual matter, and/or the container (rule 6.0B1). Despite this generous provision of the rule, it is not unusual for a sound recording to indicate *no* place of publication. Reference to rule 1.4C will help here. If the place of publication is not indicated the cataloger supplies it in square brackets, adding a question mark if necessary to indicate uncertainty. For example, the recording in Figure 8 gives no place of publication. Lacking any solid evidence, and following provisions of rule 1.4C6, the country of publication is supplied in square brackets:

```
[United States] : Stax Records ...
```

The point here is not to let the absence of a formally named place of publication cause undue concern. If desired, the cataloger can consult a standard commercial guide such as *Schwann-1, Phonolog, or Billboard...International Buyers' Guide* for information on the location of a particular publisher, should the cataloging agency deem this area to be of such importance as to warrant the extra work. Otherwise an estimate ([United States?]) will suffice. As a last resort, when not even the provable country of publication can be inferred, the abbreviation [S.l.] (for *Sine loco*) can be given.

Transcription:

I believe in you (you believe in me) / Don Davis ; [sung by] Johnnie Taylor. Stop doggin' me / B. Crutcher, D. Davis, A. Snider ; [sung by] Johnnie Taylor [sound recording].

Figure 8 - Performer in Statement of Responsibility

PUBLISHER'S NAME

6.4D2 Providing the name of the publisher can be a confusing aspect of descriptive cataloging for sound recordings. The point is to determine the name most useful to the catalog user. A common difficulty is the appearance of several similar terms in the item, thus confusing the cataloger who may be unfamiliar with the vagaries of the entertainment industry. When a recording lists the name of the publisher, a trade-name, and a series, all of which appear to be similar in nature, the cataloger must determine which name is to be preferred for this area.

There are two practical approaches. First, examine the item to see if one of the names appears in conjunction with the serial number. This is the "trade name" referred to in rule 6.4D2 and should be transcribed in the publication, etc., area. If confusion still exists because of the layout, the next approach is to consult a listing in *Phonolog* or *Schwann-1* to see how the publisher is listed there.

While sound recording series do exist, they are somewhat less common than those for other types of materials. More often, sound recording companies utilize series titles as sales gimmicks. These names (such as *Columbia Masterworks* or *Immortal Performances*) may appear on the label, but more often they appear only on the container, usually in a smaller and/or different type face from that used for the other data given. Rule 6.4D3 warns the cataloger about trade names that appear to be names of series as opposed to the name of a publishing subdivision. Care must be exercised. While *Columbia Masterworks* and *Disney Storyteller* are series, *RCA Red Seal* is not. Again, consulting a standard commercial list such as *Schwann-1* or *Phonolog* will help avoid confusion in this area.

DATES OF PUBLICATION, DISTRIBUTION, ETC.

COPYRIGHT DATES

6.4F, 1.4F6 Because of the copyright law, this can be a confusing matter for catalogers. Since 1971 by international convention the symbol ℗ has been used to indicate the copyright date of recorded sound. Because the date used is the year of first release (publication) of the recording, such dates are useful in the absence of formally stated dates of publication.

Confusion stems from the wide array of dates that might be present on labels, containers, and accompanying texts. Various © dates might be present, indicating copyright protection for the work performed, and/or the accompanying textual matter (the art work, program notes, librettos or song texts, etc.).

Because the item being cataloged is a sound recording, when a single ℗ date is present it should be transcribed as the date of copyright of the recorded sound (see Figure 9). When various ℗ dates appear on a single recording, the cataloger must determine whether they represent a reissue (as would be the case when the recording has only one work), in which case the latest date should be transcribed, or whether each date represents the copyright for a different part of the recording. In the latter instance no ℗ date should be transcribed, because there is no ℗ date that applies to the recording as a whole. An estimated date of publication can be arrived at by considering the latest date on the item to be the likely date of publication (see Figure 10).

When no ℗ date is present on the item, © dates before 1971 should be transcribed as the date of copyright (see Figure 11). For © dates later than 1970, the cataloger should infer an estimated date of publication.

WHEN NO COPYRIGHT DATE IS PRESENT

AACR 2 requires a date of publication, distribution, release, etc., to be given in every description. When no copyright dates are present on sound recordings, the cataloger, exercising great care, may estimate the date of release in one of two ways.

First, it is reasonable to assume that a recent LP recording was released within one year of the date it was recorded, although this is not always a reliable yardstick, because many recordings are released years after their performance. This is not a reasonable approach with most compact disc recordings, however, because many are re-releases of earlier LP discs. Furthermore, delays in production of compact discs might contribute to a greater than usual time lag between date of recording and date of release. However, when the date of recording is within the current twelve months, this method may be applied with either type of commercially released recording.

MMG-1118
(MMG-1118A)   SIDE 1

**AGES OF SONG
MARTIN BEST**
1. JOG ON/CARMAN'S WHISTLE 3:12
2. THE FRYAR AND THE NUN/NEW NOTHING 2:00
3. O MISTRESS MINE 3:52
4. ALMAINE 1:58
5. BONNY SWEET ROBIN/ROBIN HOOD AND THE TANNER 3:00
6. NIGHT PEECE KEMP'S JEGGE 1:35
7. THE WILLOW SONG 4:06
8. FAREWELL, DEAR LOVE
9. WHEN DAFFODILS BEGIN TO PE...

Ⓟ 1979 EMI Records (UK)

THE MOSS MUSIC GROUP (CANADA) INC.   SIDE 2

**AGES OF SONG
MARTIN BEST**
1. WHERE THE BEE SUCKS 2:20
2. FIFE TUNE AND LAST BALLETT 1:34
3. COME AWAY DEATH 3:34
4. WHEN THAT I WAS A LITTLE TINY BOY 2:58
5. SOUNDS AND SWEET AYRES 11:93

Ⓟ 1979 EMI Records (UK)

notes © MARTIN BEST, 1979

*Front cover: The 'Chandos' portrait of Shakespeare (artist unknown).
Courtesy: National Portrait Gallery. Photo of Martin Best: Tony Russell. Design: Robert Claxton.*

Recording Producer: NICK INGMAN
Balance Engineer: PETER VINCE
Ⓟ *1979, EMI Records Ltd.*

THE MOSS MUSIC GROUP, INC.,
48 W. 38th ST., N.Y., N.Y. 10018

DIGI 101
(T-101B)   Side 2
                                                (16:46)

DIGITAL HITS OF 1740
ALBINONI: Adagio (7:41)
Cambridge Chamber Orchestra: Rolf Smedvig
J.S. BACH: Jesu, Joy of Man's Desiring (2:54)
Cambridge Chamber Orchestra: Empire Brass Quintet
MOURET: Randeau (from Symphony of Fanfares) (1:33)
Empire Brass Quintet
J.S. BACH: Brandenburg Concerto #2, Movement 3 (2:44)
Cambridge Chamber Orchestra: soloists: Emanuel Borok, violin;
Paul Fried, flute, Alfred Genovese, oboe: Rolf Smedvig, trumpet

                                                Side 1
                                                (17:41)
DIGITAL HITS OF 1740
PACHELBEL: Canon (5:57)
Cambridge Chamber Orchestra
Concerto in F for Trumpet and Strings
First movement (2:05)
Second movement (1:08)
Third movement (3:11)
...er Orchestra: Rolf Smedvig, solo trumpet
...LI: Giga (from Opus 5) (2:28)
Empire Brass Quintet
Rondeau (1:31) and Badinerie (0:52)
Chamber Orchestra: Rolf Smedvig,
solo trumpet
Ⓟ 1979, DigiTech

Figure 9 - © and Ⓟ Dates

current twelve months, this method may be applied with either type of commercially released recording.

The other approach is even less reliable, but still worth mentioning. The cataloger can check a manufacturer's number file to see if there is a chronological pattern among recordings within a range of serial numbers. Large files of this type are available in all major network union catalogs. Be advised, however, that many record manufaturers do not assign these so-called "serial" numbers serially, so this approach should be used only as a last resort. A date may be estimated this way only when a clear chronological pattern is present in the file.

If all else fails, especially with older recordings, discographies might be of some help.

RECORD FOUR

Side 7

INCLUDING THE LAST RECORDINGS
WIDOR: TOCCATA IN F MAJOR
from the FIFTH ORGAN SYMPHONY. OP.42
MacDOWELL: A. D. 1620 from *SEA PIECES*. OP. 55, No 3
SOUSA: THE STARS AND STRIPES FOREVER
BACH: SINFONIA to CANATA. BMW 29:
"Wir danken dir, Gott wir danken dir (We thank Thee, Lord, we
The Gewandhaus Orchestra of Leipzig; Hans-Joachim Rotzsch, Conductor
REMARKS MADE BY MR. BIGGS AT RADIO CITY
MUSIC HALL ON MARCH 2, 1973

Side 8

RELEASED FOR THE FIRST TIME
HANDEL: FROM THE *AYLESFORD* PIECES
Fuga • Impertinence • Aria • Concerto
Minuet in G Minor • Minuet in F Major • Minuet in D Minor
Minuet in D Major • Gavotte • Minuet in B-flat Major
Minuet in B-flat Major • Minuet in D Major

Figure 10 - Various Ⓟ Dates

This album contains previously released material

© 1979 CBS Inc./ Ⓟ 1972, 1973, 1974, 1975, 1976, 1979 CBS Inc.
Warning: All rights reserved. Unauthorized duplication is a violatio

---

an exquisitely played encore performance of a Bach saraband ..."
  - Roy M. Close
    © 1979, Minneapolis Star & Tribune
    All rights reserved

Figure 11 - © Dates Only

Producer: Miloslav Kuba
Engineers: M. Kulhan (Richter), F. Burda (Benda)
Recorded October 27, 1955 (Richter)
and September 25-27, 1956 (Benda)
at Studio Domovina, Prague
Winner of Grand Prix du Disque, 1961.
By arrangement with Supraphon.
Executive Producer: Steven Vining
Remastering Engineer: Robert McNabb
Cover Art: M. Patrick
Art Director: Meredythe Jones Rossi
Ⓟ A product of Pickwick International, Inc.
Pickwick Records Division
7500 Excelsior Blvd., Minneapolis, MN 55426
© 1979, Pickwick International, Inc. Printed in U.S.A.
Distribué au Canada par / Distributed in Canada by
Pickwick Records of Canada, Ltd.
106-108 McMaster Ave., Ajax, Ontario, Canada L1S-2E7
Warning: Unauthorized reproduction of this recording is
prohibited by applicable laws and subject to criminal prosecution.
This recording has been previously released.
Library of Congress Card Catalog Number: 79-750374

PHYSICAL DESCRIPTION AREA

TYPES OF SCORES

5.5B1   Given below are the definitions from the *AACR 2* "Glossary" for the types of scores and parts most commonly found in library collections. One should bear in mind that the bibliographic use of terminology as advocated in *AACR 2* does not necessarily coincide with the colloquial use of the same terms. For example, the word "score" is commonly used in everyday speech to indicate *any* type of printed music.

When attempting to choose the appropriate term keep in mind the basic definition of the word "score" as given below. The most basic requirement is that the score represent all of the different parts, i.e. *more than one* instrument or voice. A work for one instrument or one voice cannot be rendered in score.

> SCORE.   A series of staves on which all the different instrumental and/or vocal parts of a musical work are written, one under the other in vertical alignment, so that the parts may be read simultaneously.

> CONDENSED SCORE.   A musical score giving only the principal musical parts on a minimum number of staves generally organised by instrumental section.

> CLOSE SCORE.   A musical score giving all the parts on a minimum number of staves, normally two, as with hymns.

> MINIATURE SCORE.   A musical score not primarily intended for performance use, with type reduced in size.

> PIANO [VIOLIN, ETC.] CONDUCTOR PART [SCORE].   A performance part for a particular instrument of an ensemble to which cues have been added for the other instruments to permit the performer of the part also to conduct the performance.

> VOCAL SCORE.   A score showing all vocal parts, with accompaniment, if any, arranged for keyboard instrument.

> PIANO SCORE.   A reduction of an orchestral score to a version for piano on two staves.

> CHORUS SCORE.   A score of a vocal work showing only the chorus parts, with accompaniment, if any, arranged for keyboard instrument.

> PART (MUSIC).   The music for one of the participating voices or instruments in a musical work; the written or printed copy of such a part for the use of a performer, designated in the physical description area by the word *part*.

> (*AACR 2* p. 564-572)

Advice on the use of the terms "chorus score" and "vocal score" is available in a Library of Congress Music Cataloging Decision.

> **MCD**   In using the terms "chorus score" and "vocal score" in the physical description area, be governed by the following clarifications of the definitions of these terms in Appendix D:

Chorus score. This term is used only for works originally for solo voice(s) and chorus with accompaniment. In order for this term to be used in the physical description area for a particular manifestation of a work, the item must omit the solo voice(s), at least in those portions of the work in which the chorus does not sing. In addition, if the accompaniment is originally for other than keyboard instrument it must be omitted. (Understand "if any" to mean "omitted or.") This term is not used for works originally unaccompanied or for any manifestation of an accompanied work with the original accompaniment.

Vocal score. This term is used for works originally for chorus and/or one or more solo voices with accompaniment. In order for this term to be used in the physical description area for a particular manifestation of a work, the item must include the solo voice(s) (if any). In addition, if the accompaniment is originally for other than keyboard instrument it must be omitted. (Understand "if any" in the definition to mean "omitted or.") This term is not used for works originally unaccompanied or for any manifestation of an accompanied work with the original accompaniment.

If neither "chorus score," "close score," nor "vocal score" applies to a vocal publication, use "score" or "miniature score" (unless the item is for unaccompanied solo voice or unaccompanied unison voices). (*MCB* 12:6:2-3)

POPULAR MUSIC FOLIOS

Notice that "vocal score" applies only when the music was originally written for orchestra and now appears in a version for piano and voice(s). Because music in the popular idiom cannot be said to have been written for any particular medium of performance (let alone voice(s) and orchestra), a popular music folio (or a single song for that matter) cannot be said to be a "vocal score." Describe such publications as "1 score."

EXTENT OF ITEM

SCORES AND PARTS

5.5B1 MCD While the specific material designation terms listed following the first paragraph of this rule (score, condensed score, etc.) are to be applied to entire physical units, this is not true of the phrase "of music" in the third paragraph. When "of music" is used, apply the phrase only to those sequences (for the definition of "sequence" see 2.5B2, footnote 2) which are, or consist primarily of, music, and not to sequences which are primarily text.

> 1 score (vi, 27 p.)
>   (*only p. 1-27 are music*)
>
> 129 p. of music, [7] p.
>   (*only p. 1-129 are music*)

but

> xxv p., 55 p. of music
>   (*only p. 1-55 are music*)
>
> 46, 39 p. of music
>   (*both sequences are music*)

Do not use "sheet" in describing music. Describe leaves printed on one side only in terms of leaves, whether they are bound, folded, or separate. (*MCB* 13:10:2-3)

5.5B3 The following Library of Congress Rule Interpretation gives instruction for providing the pagination of a single part, and for indicating the extent of scores and parts in volumes:

RI   When there is only one part, include its pagination. (Disregard the second example under 5.5D1.)

```
1 score (20 p.) + 1 part (3 p.)
```

When parts are issued in two or more "volumes," include the number of volumes.

```
1 score (2 v.) + 1 part (2 v.)
1 score (3 v.) + 2 parts (3 v.)
4 parts (6 v.)
```

(*CSB* 33:34)

The volume designation would be applicable to a situation where a collection of works in score and part format is issued in multiple volumes. In the first two examples each volume has a score (probably bound) and parts (at the back or in a pocket). In the third example four parts are issued in each of the six volumes (probably contained in a pocket in each volume).

Other configurations are possible. A single string quartet, issued as parts for the violins, viola, and violoncello would be described as:

```
4 parts.
```

A piano trio, with a score for the pianist, and one part each for the violin and violoncello, would be described as:

```
1 score (32 p.) + 2 parts.
```

Note that no pagination is given when more than one part is present.

If the item being cataloged is a score and set of parts for orchestral performance, only the number of unique parts is given. For example, a symphony for string orchestra, with multiple copies of parts for violin, viola, violoncello, and double bass, would be described as:

```
1 score (79 p.) + 5 parts.
```

The number of multiple copies of each part would be considered local holdings information, and could be noted in the local bibliographic record (rule 5.7B20). More often such information is given on"parts cards" filed in the shelf list (see Figure 12), or is contained in the local library's circulation and holdings records.

Parts	Instrument	Parts	Instrument	Parts	Instrument	Parts	Instrument
							Total Parts
	Score-full Score-piano		Sax, Alto Sax, Tenor Sax, Baritone		Cornet I Cornet II Cornet III		Harp I Harp II Organ Piano Celesta Harpsichord
	Piccolo Flute I Flute II Flute III		Bassoon I Bassoon II Contrabassoon		Trombone I Trombone II Trombone III		Violin I Violin II Violin III Viola Violoncello Cello-bass Double-bass
	Oboe I Oboe II Oboe III English Horn		Horn I Horn II Horn III Horn IV		Euphonium Tuba		
	Clarinet, Eb Clarinet I Clarinet II Clarinet III		Trumpet I Trumpet II Trumpet III		Percussion Tympani Bells, Chimes Mallet Perc. Electronic Instr.		Solo Instrument Vocal Parts
	Basset-horn Clarinet, Alto Clarinet, Bass Clarinet, Contra						SMH-30-76

Figure 12 - Parts Card

SOUND RECORDINGS

6.5B1 MCD For multipart items, give only the number of physical units (e.g., discs) in the physical description area. If the number of containers or discographic units (often called "volumes") differs from the number of physical units give this information in notes (cf. MCD 6.7B10, MCD 6.7B18 [below]). (*MCB* 14:12:3)

TOTAL PLAYING TIME

6.5B2 RI When the total playing time of a sound recording is not stated on the item but the durations of its parts (sides, individual works, etc.) are, if desired add the stated durations together and record the total, rounding off to the next minute if the total exceeds 5 minutes.

Precede a statement of duration by "ca." only if the statement is given on the item in terms of an approximation. Do not add "ca." to a duration arrived at by adding partial durations or by rounding off seconds.

If no durations are stated on the item or if the durations of some but not all parts of a work are stated, do not give a statement of duration. Do not approximate durations from the number of sides of a disc, type of cassette, etc. (*CSB* 33:36)

MCD Apply the first paragraph of RI 6.5B2, above, and give the total duration in the physical description area if the recording contains only one work (as defined in 25.26B[1]) regardless of the number of physical units (e.g., discs) in the recording. (*MCB* 12:10:3)
State the duration in the form illustrated by the examples in rule 6.5B2. (*MCB* 13:8:3)

OTHER PHYSICAL DETAILS FOR SOUND RECORDINGS

According to changes forthcoming in the consolidated reprinting of *AACR 2*, a new first element of other physical details has been added to accommodate description of digital audio recordings. This has been accomplished by requiring that the first element in this area describe the way in which the sound is encoded on the item being cataloged, thus giving the user an idea of what type of playback equipment will be required.

For standard grooved discs, for which a turntable with a needle is required for playback, give the term "analog." For compact discs requiring a laser device for playback give the word "digital." Give other physical details as noted in the printed text of *AACR 2*, preceded by a comma-space. No playing speed is given for digital discs because it is not a playback requirement. The size of the standard compact digital audio disc is 4 3/4 in. These instructions are outlined in detail in *CSB* 30:24-27.

```
1 sound disc (50 min.) : analog, 33 1/3 rpm, stereo. ; 12 in.

1 sound disc (45 min.) : digital ; 4 3/4 in.
```

6.5C3 MCD "For tape cassettes, give the playing speed only if it is stated on the item." (*MCB* 15:7:3)

6.5C7 MCD When the number of sound channels is not stated explicitly, do not record any term, e.g.,

```
1 sound disc (ca. 49 min.) : analog, 33 1/3 rpm ; 12 in.
```

(*MCB* 12:3:2)

6.5C8 MCD Apply this option whenever the information would be needed for selecting playback equipment to get the full audio effect of the recording; e.g., record the quadrophonic process when special equipment is required to listen to the recording in quad., even if it can be listened to in stereo. without the special equipment, e.g.,

```
1 sound disc (ca. 57 min.) : analog, 33 1/3 rpm, quad. QS ; 12 in.
```

(*MCB* 12:3:2)

ACCOMPANYING MATERIAL

1.5E1 MCD   Normally consider options c and d to be mutually exclusive with regard to a specific item of accompanying material. If the need is felt to give more information about accompanying material than can be given under option d (including "Optional addition"), describe the material in a note and omit it from the physical description area. (In the second sentence of 6.7B11, the phrase "not mentioned in the physical description area" modifies "accompanying material," not "details.") (*MCB* 12:6:2)

SERIES AREA

Series found on music materials are not substantially different from those found on other types of publications. Two minor caveats apply, however. First, do not confuse a publisher's number on a printed music publication with a series statement (see PLATE AND PUBLISHER'S NUMBER, below). Likewise, do not confuse a sound recording manufacturer's trade name with a series statement (see above under PLACE OF PUBLICATION AND NAME OF PUBLISHER FOR SOUND RECORDINGS).

NOTES AREA

ORDER OF NOTES

The lists below are intended to serve as a guide for the order of notes in bibliographic records for music materials. Remember that many of these notes are used only to explain or otherwise elucidate information contained in the preceding areas of the description. Note that the order in both lists is essentially the same with the exception of the manufacturer's number, which appears first for sound recordings, according to a Library of Congress Rule Interpretation (see below).

Music

Form of composition and medium of performance (5.7B1)

Text (language of sung or spoken text) (5.7B2)

Source of title proper (5.7B3)

Variations in title (5.7B4)

Parallel titles and other title information (5.7B5)

Statements of responsibility (5.7B6)

Edition and history (5.7B7)

Notation (5.7B8)

Publication, distribution, etc. (5.7B9)

Duration of performance (5.7B10)

Accompanying material (5.7B11)

Series (5.7B12)

Dissertation note (5.7B13)

Audience (5.7B14)

Contents (5.7B18)

Publishers' numbers and plate numbers (5.7B19)

Copy described and library's holdings (5.7B20)

Sound Recordings

Manufacturer's number (6.7B19)

Nature or artistic form and medium of performance (6.7B1)

Text (language of sung or spoken text) (6.7B2)

Source of title proper (6.7B3)

Variations in title (6.7B4)

Parallel titles and other title information (6.7B5)

Statements of responsibility (6.7B6)

Edition and history (6.7B7)

Publication, distribution, etc. (6.7B10)

Accompanying material (6.7B11)

Series (6.7B12)

Dissertation note (6.7B13)

Audience (6.7B14)

Other formats available (6.7B16)

Summary (6.7B17) (spoken word recordings only)

Contents (6.7B18)

Copy described and library's holdings (6.7B20)

NOTES FOR PRINTED MUSIC

FORM OF COMPOSITION AND MEDIUM OF PERFORMANCE

5.7B1 MCD   Do not name the medium of performance in a note if it is implied by the title or other title information (e.g., "Chorale prelude;" "Kaddish : symphony") or by the musical form stated in a note made under this rule (e.g., "Opera in two acts"; "Ballet").

If an item is described in the physical description area as "chorus score" or "vocal score" (cf. the decision of 5.5B1 above), give in a note the original medium of performance and the instrument for which the accompaniment is arranged (or indicate that the accompaniment is omitted) if this information is not clear from the rest of the description.

```
For solo voices (SATB), and orchestra; acc. arr. for piano

For chorus (TTBB) and band; without the acc.
```

(*MCB* 12:6:3; rev. 15:7:3)

Also apply this provision to other works that are arrangements.

```
Originally for string quartet

Acc. arr. for piano
```

LANGUAGE OF SUNG OR SPOKEN TEXT

5.7B2   The language of the words of a vocal work should be indicated in a note whenever it is not clear from the content of the preceding description. This note is governed by a general Library of Congress Rule Interpretation.

1.7B2 RI   Generally restrict the making of language and script notes to the situations covered in this directive. (Note: In this statement, "language" and "language of the item" mean the language or languages of the content of the item (e.g., for books the language of the text; [for music the language of the words that are to be sung or spoken]); "title data" means title proper and other title information.)

If the language of the item is not clear from the transcription of the title data, make a note naming the language whether or not the language is named after a uniform title. Use "and" in all cases to link two languages (or the final two when more than two are named). If more than one language is named, give the predominant language first if readily apparent; name the other languages in alphabetical order. For the form of the name of the language, follow *Library of Congress Subject Headings*. (*Exception*: Use "Greek" for classical Greek and modern Greek. If, however, the item is a translation from classical Greek into modern Greek, use "Modern Greek" in the note. If the item includes text in both, use "Classical Greek" and "Modern Greek" in the note.) For some "dialects" that cannot be established as subject headings, a specific language will be used in the note area only. (see RI 25.5D [below] for the use of language names in uniform titles) ... (*CSB* 30:9)

When all of the words appear in more than one language, use "and" to link the languages in the note.

```
French and English words

English, German, and Russian words
```

If the words are in more than one language (one verse in French, the rest in English), use "or" to link the languages in the note.

```
English or French words
```

If desired, indicate in a note the words that are also printed separately in textual format (usually in addition to being printed between the staves in the score).

```
German words; English translation printed also as text
```

DURATION OF PERFORMANCE

5.7B10   This information should be given only if stated in the item being cataloged. Such statements may occur at the beginning or ending of the music, on the title page, in the preliminaries, or on the cover. Sometimes the duration of each movement will be printed at the end of each movement. These may be added together to derive the note. Do not attempt to infer the duration of performance from metronome markings, etc.

5.7B10 MCD   In a statement of duration in the note area, separate the digits representing hours, minutes, and seconds by colons. If a duration is expressed in seconds only, precede it by a colon.

```
Duration: 15:30

Duration: 1:25:00

Duration: :45
```

Precede a statement of duration in the note area by "ca." only if the statement is given on the item in terms of an approximation.

```
Duration: ca. 27:00

Duration: ca. 1:10:00
```

(*MCB* 13:8:3)

CONTENTS

5.7B18   Contents notes can be very important to catalog users seeking a particular work (especially a song) in a collection. The instructions at rule 5.7B18 cover the specific case of a collection of works, all in the same musical form which is named in the title area of the description. In such cases, give only the other details (opus or thematic catalog numbering, key, etc.) in the contents note.

```
Flute concertos / Wolfgang Amadeus Mozart ...
Contents: No. 1 in G, K. 313 -- No. 2 in D, K. 314
```

It is especially important to give complete contents for popular music folios.

```
Vocal selections from Hair ...
Contents: Aquarius -- Donna -- Ain't got no -- Air -- I got life
-- Hair -- Easy to be hard -- Frank Mills -- Where do I go? -- What a
piece of work is man -- Good morning starshine -- Let the sunshine in
```

```
Separate lives, Burning heart & 10 knockout hits ...
    Contents: Separate lives / words and music by Stephen Bishop --
Burning heart / words and music by Jim Peterik and Frankie Sullivan --
Lonely ol' night / words and music by John Mellencamp -- You belong to
the city / words and music by Glenn Frey and Jack Tempchin -- Crazy for
you / words and music by Jon Lind and John Bettis -- Broken wings /
words and music by Richard Page, Steve George, and John Lang -- Girls
are more fun / words and music by Ray Parker, Jr. -- Never / words and
music by Holly Knight, Gene Bloch, Ann Wilson, and Nancy Wilson -- Can't
fight this feeling / words and music by Kevin Cronin -- Never ending
story / words and music by Giorgio Moroder and Keith Forsey -- Saving
all my love for you / words by Gerry Goffin ; music by Michael Masser
-- The search is over / words and music by Frank Sullivan and Jim
Peterik
```

It is also traditional to make a contents note for a work in many movements if the movements have distinctive titles (e.g., a suite).

```
La mer / Claude Debussy ....
    Contents: De l'aube à midi sur la mer -- Jeux de vagues -- Dialogue
du vent et de la mer
```

PLATE AND PUBLISHER'S NUMBER

5.7B19   Plate numbers and publisher's numbers can be crucial for bibliographic identification of editions and states, and sometimes for dating printed music. Publisher's numbers are also critical information for ordering printed music, because few music publishers participate in the ISBN program. The following Library of Congress policy statements define plate and publisher's numbers, and clarify the provisions of rule 5.7B19.

5.7B19 MCD   In applying this rule, be governed by the following definitions:

> *Plate number.*   A serial number assigned to a publication by a music publisher, usually printed at the bottom of each plate and sometimes appearing also on the title page. If initials, abbreviations, or words identifying a publisher appear with the number, consider them a part of it. If an additional number, corresponding to the title number of pages or plates, follows the plate number (often after a dash), do not consider it part of the plate number.

> *Publisher's number.*   A number similar to a plate number but not appearing on each page of the publication. It may appear on the title page, the cover, and/or the first page of music. (*MCB* 13:1:4)

RI   Transcribe a publisher's number even if a plate number is also transcribed. Transcribe the statement as it appears even if this means giving again a publisher's name already transcribed in the publication, distribution, etc. area.

```
Publisher's no.: Edition Peters Nr. 8444
```

When transcribing two or more distinct numbers, give each in a separate note. (Follow the rule as written for the transcription of numbers for an item in multiple volumes.) Transcribe a publisher's number before a plate number. (*CSB* 33:34)

MCD   When a designation such as "no." "Nr." "cat. no.," "Ed. Nr.", etc., appears with a publisher's number or plate number, do not consider it to be part of the number and do not transcribe it. If, however, initials, abbreviations, or words identifying the publisher also appear with the number, follow the instructions in RI 5.7B19 and transcribe the entire statement as it appears.

On item: Cat. no. 01 6516
Note: Publisher's no.: 01 6510

On item: Nr. 3892
Note: Publisher's no.: 3892

     but:

On item: Edition Peters Nr. 3891
Note: Publisher's no.: Edition Peters Nr. 3891

(*MCB* 16:12:5)

COPY BEING DESCRIBED AND LIBRARY'S HOLDINGS

5.7B20 MCD   The following Library of Congress Music Cataloging Decision reflects LC internal policy: "Notes made under this rule will be considered local information and will not appear on printed cards or be displayed in an automated record." (*MCB* 12:3:2)

NOTES FOR SOUND RECORDINGS

PUBLISHER'S (I.E., LABEL NAME AND) NUMBER

6.7B19 RI   When applying rule 6.7B19 to include the label name and number in a note, make this note the first one. Transcribe spaces and hyphens in publisher's numbers on sound recordings as they appear. Separate the first and last numbers of a sequence by a dash (two hyphens).

     Angel: S 37781

     RCA Red Seal: ARL1-3715

     Deutsche Harmonia Mundi: 1C 065-99 615

     Euphonic: EES-101--EES-102

When the item bears both a set number and numbers for the individual items (e.g., discs), give only the set number unless it does not appear on the individual items; in that case give the set number first, followed by the numbers of the individual items in parentheses.

     Philips: 6769 042 (9500 718--9500 719)

Give matrix numbers only if they are the only numbers shown on the item. Follow each matrix number by the word *matrix* in parentheses.

     Melodiіa : C10 06767 (matrix)--C10 06768 (matrix)

(*CSB* 14:17)

MCD   When a publisher's number appears in various forms on a sound recording, its container, accompanying material, etc., transcribe first the form on the recording itself (e.g., the labels of a disc), followed in parentheses by the other variant(s), each preceded by a statement showing its location.

     Angel: S-37337 (on container: DS 37337)

When two or more distinct publisher's numbers on a sound recording, its container, accompanying material, etc., transcribe each in a separate note. Follow each number other than the first by an indication of its location, if appropriate.

```
Page: FSM 43721

Page: POPR 790051 (on container)
```

If, however, each unit (e.g., disc) in a set bears an individual number but the item also bears a number applying to the set as a whole, follow the instructions in RI 6.7B19.

(*MCB* 16:3:4)

PERFORMER NOTES

6.7B6, 1.7A3 These are "statements of responsibility" notes. Transcribe them from the item and use prescribed punctuation as outlined for the statement of responsibility area. Do not give a performer note for a multi-performer collection with a collective title. In this case, give the performers' names in the contents note (rule 6.7B18) in parentheses, following titles and/or statements of responsibility for each work performed.

DATA ON RECORDING SESSIONS, EDITION, AND HISTORY

6.7B7 These data are referred to under the heading "Edition and history" in *AACR 2*. Information on the recording sessions can be used for discographical purposes to identify particular performances that may have been released at different times on different labels or in different physical formats. Whenever information on the recording session is indicated in the item, it should be given in an "edition and history" note.

```
    Recorded Oct. 27, 1955 (1st work), and Sept. 25-27, 1956 (2nd work),
at Studio Domovina, Prague
```

This note is also used to indicate that recorded material has been issued before.

```
    "All selections previously released"
```


PHYSICAL DESCRIPTION -- CONTAINERS

6.7B10 MCD Give a note on the presence of container(s) only when the number of containers is not clear from the rest of the description. (*MCB* 12:3:2)

PHYSICAL DESCRIPTION -- DURATIONS

6.7B10 RI If the individual works in a collection are identified in the title and statement of responsibility area, list the durations of the works in a note. If the individual works are listed in a contents note (6.7B18), give their durations there.

When recording individual durations in the note area, give them as they appear on the item (e.g., in minutes and seconds if so stated). If only the durations of the parts of a work are stated (e.g., the movements of a sonata), if desired, add the stated durations together and record the total for the work in minutes, rounding off to the next minute.

Precede a statement of duration by "ca." only if the statement is given on the item in terms of an approximation. Do not add "ca." to a duration arrived at by adding up partial durations or by rounding off seconds.

If the duration of a work is not stated on the item, or if the durations of some but not all of the parts are stated, do not give a statement of duration for that work. Do not approximate durations from the number of sides of a disc, type of cassette, etc. (*CSB* 13:14-15)

MCD   In a statement of duration in the note area, separate the digits representing hours, minutes and seconds by colons. If a duration is expressed in seconds only, precede it by a colon.

```
Duration: 45:00

Durations: 1:25:00; :48; 15:10

Duration: ca. 1:15:00

Durations: ca. 27:00; ca. 17:00
```

(*MCB* 13:8:4; rev. 15:7:3)

ACCOMPANYING MATERIAL

6.7B11 MCD   Make notes on accompanying program notes, etc., only if they are significant. (*MCB* 15:7:3)

Program notes are ubiquitous on sound recording containers. Frequently they have little useful information. Consider program notes to be significant only when they are substantial (e.g., a separate booklet, score, libretto, etc.) or when they provide information that is unique, such as a discography, or historical or biographical information that cannot be found in standard reference sources. Do not consider the mere presence of textual matter on a container to be sufficiently significant to warrant making a note.

See also the Music Cataloging Decision under ACCOMPANYING MATERIAL, 1.5E1, above.

OTHER FORMATS AVAILABLE

6.7B16 RI   Generally make a note on the availability of the item in another medium or another media, if this is known. Record these notes in the position of 6.7B16 ... and use the term "issued."

```
Issued also as motion picture, filmstrip, and slide set
```

(*CSB* 13:15)

CONTENTS

6.7B18   Contents notes are very important for musical sound recordings, most of which are collections. Information about the individual selections on a recording is essential when the recording collection cannot be browsed. Therefore, complete contents should always be given when the recording has a collective title.

When contents are given, durations of the individual works (if present on the item) should be given in parentheses following the descriptive information for each work. Two Library of Congress policy statements apply to the inclusion of durations in contents notes.

RI   For durations of works recorded in a formal contents note, apply RI 6.7B10 [above]. (*MCB* 12:10:2)

MCD   For the forms of durations recorded in a formal contents note, see MCD 6.7B10, above. (*MCB* 13:8:4)

> ```
> Pleasure songs for flute [sound recording] ...
> Contents: Passepied from Suite de Ballet / Vaughan Williams
> (2:02) -- Greensleeves (4:40) -- Molly on the shore / Grainger
> (4:13) ...
> ```

The provisions of rule 5.7B18 also apply to sound recordings. That is, if all the works on a sound recording that is a collection are in the same musical form and that musical form is named in the title area of the description, give only the other details in the contents note.

> ```
> Six sonatas for flute and harpsichord [sound recording] / Carl
> Philipp Emanuel Bach ...
> Contents: No. 1 in B flat major, Wq. 125 (6:14) -- No. 2 in D
> major, Wq. 126 (6:26) -- No. 3 in G major, Wq. 127 (7:01) ...
> ```

When each performer on a collective sound recording performs a different selection, each name is given in parentheses following the transcription for the work performed.

> ```
> A Motown anniversary collection [sound recording] ...
> Contents: Heat wave / E. Holland, L. Dozier, B. Holland (Martha
> Reeves & The Vandellas) -- You've really got a hold on me / W.
> Robinson, Jr. (The Miracles) -- Signed, sealed, delivered / Stevie
> Wonder, S. Wright, L.M. Hardaway, L. Garrett (Stevie Wonder) ...
> ```

MCD   For multipart items, when the number of discographic units (often called "volumes" by publishers) differs from the number of physical units (e.g., discs) or containers, include when necessary the number of physical units or containers in the contents note (cf. RI 2.7B18 (3) (6[d]) [*CSB 25:40*]).

> ```
> Contents:  1. Vom 6. Sonntag bis zum 17. Sonntag nach Trinitatis (6
> discs) -- 2. Vom 18. bis zum 27. Sonntag nach Trinitatis (6 discs)
> ...
> ```

(*MCB* 14:12:3)

CHAPTER 2: CHOICE AND FORM OF ENTRY

CHOICE OF ENTRY

The basic rule for choice of entry is applicable to all types of materials. That is, " enter ... under the heading for the personal author ... the principal personal author ... or the probable personal author." (*AACR 2* 21.1a1) Composers of music, and in some cases performers as well, are considered to be the authors of the works they create. For this reason the only special rules for music materials in chapter 21 are those for modifications of works (rules 21.18-21.22), sound recordings (rule 21.23), and related works such as cadenzas and librettos (rule 21.28). The rules for modifications of works are all fairly straightforward and require no particular explanation. Library of Congress rule interpretations and cataloging decisions concerning related works are discussed briefly below. The rules for sound recordings, however, are somewhat confusing and receive special attention below.

ADAPTATIONS AND ADDED ACCOMPANIMENTS

21.18C MCD   For a musical work adapted by its original composer see MCD 25.26B (under UNIFORM TITLES) below. (*MCB* 13:9:1)

21.21 MCD   For uniform titles, additional added entries, subject headings and classification for works with added accompaniments, etc., see MCD 25.31B2 (under UNIFORM TITLES below). (*MCB* 14:1:3)

CADENZAS AND LIBRETTOS

21.28 A cadenza is a passage inserted near the end of a concerto movement that is intended to display the technical accomplishments of the solo performer. Though sometimes improvised, cadenzas also are composed and published, sometimes by the concerto's composer, sometimes by a virtuoso performer. The difficulty in choice of entry is that the cadenza almost always will be used in conjunction with another composition, so it might or might not commonly be sought under its own heading.

In keeping with the basic rule (21.1), rule 21.28 directs entry of a related work under its own heading. A Library of Congress Music Cataloging Decision reminds us that a cadenza is always a related work:

21.28A MCD Treat cadenzas as related works under this rule whether they are composed by the composer of the works into which they are to be interpolated or by someone else.

```
Mozart,  Wolfgang Amadeus
   [Cadenzas, piano.  Selections]
   Trente-cinq points d'orgue pour le piano-forte / composés
par W.A. Mozart et se rapportant à ses concertos ...
```
(Added entry: Mozart, Wolgang Amadeus. Concertos, piano, orchestra. Selections)

```
Backhaus,  Wilhelm
   Kadenz sum Rondo des C-Dur Konzers von Beethoven / von
Wilhelm Backhaus ...
```
(Added entry: Beethoven, Ludwig von. Concertos, piano, orchestra, no. 1, op. 15, C major. Rondo)

(*MCB* 13: 7 : 1-2)

21.28A, ftnt 7 For librettos the Library of Congress has chosen to apply the alternative rule 21.28, in footnote 7, entering them under the heading appropriate to the musical work.

MCD In order for a libretto to qualify for entry "under the heading appropriate to the musical work" (footnote 7), a reference to the libretto's musical setting must appear in the chief source of information or in the foreword or other prefatory matter of the publication. (*MCB* 14: 12: 4)

SOUND RECORDINGS

In choosing the main entry for a sound recording, the process of assigning responsibility for the intellectual content is somewhat more complex. *AACR 2* has introduced main entry under performer -- a new concept in library cataloging -- although recognition of the performer's creative role is not in itself a new musical concept. Nevertheless, performers may be designated as the main entry by virtue of their activities as writers (i.e., composers, etc.), interpreters, and/or players.

21.23A-B The first consideration in choice of entry for sound recordings is the content of the recording. If the recording contains works by the same person(s) or body (bodies), then main entry is determined as it would be for the same works in their printed manifestations. For example, a recording that contains only a performance of *String quartet no. 13 in G major, op. 106* by Antonín Dvořák, is entered under the heading for Dvořák because it is a recording of one work by one person (21.23A). Likewise, a recording that contains performances of *Romeo and Juliet* and *Francesco da Rimini* by Tchaikovsky is entered under the heading for Tchaikovsky because it is a recording of two works by the same person (21.23B).

6.1G If, according to rule 6.1G, separate descriptions were made for each musical work on a collective sound recording that lacks a collective title, each separate description would be entered under the heading appropriate to the work described, the collective nature of the recording being disregarded. (See also above, under SOUND RECORDINGS DESCRIBED AS A UNIT.)

21.23C If a sound recording contains works by two or more different persons (do not confuse this with the provisions for joint authorship, for which apply rules 21.23A-B and 21.6), the choice of main entry is dependent first upon whether or not a collective title is present in the description. If there is a collective title, the main entry is under the heading for the principal performer or the first of two or three principal performers. If there are four or more principal performers, or no principal performers, main entry is under the collective title. A Library of Congress Rule Interpretation clarifies these provisions, and includes a variety of examples illustrating the most common situations.

PRINCIPAL PERFORMER

21.23C RI In applying the rules and these interpretations, understand "performer" to mean a person or corporate body whose performance is heard on the sound recording. When a person performs as a member of a corporate body, do not consider him or her as a separate person to be a performer. However, do not consider a conductor or accompanist to be a member of the body he or she conducts or accompanies. If a person's name appears in conjunction with the name of a group, determine whether the corporate name includes this personal name. If the conclusion is that the corporate name does not include the person's name, do not consider the person a member of the group; if the conclusion is that it does include the person's name, consider the person to be a member of the group.

For recordings containing musical works by different composers or writers, follow the guidelines below in 1) deciding whether or not there are principal performers and 2) identifying the principal performers, if any.

The use of the term "principal performer" in 21.23C-D can lead to confusion since the term implies a performer who is more important (or, in the words of footnote 5 on *AACR 2* p. 314, given greater prominence) than other performers. This interpretation, however, would often produce undesirable results: it would make main entry under the heading for a performer impossible under 21.23C when there is only one performer or when there are only two or three performers who are given equal prominence. To avoid this difficulty, apply the following:

> When two or more performers are named in the chief source of information, consider to be principal performers those given the greatest prominence there. If all the performers named in the chief source of information are given equal prominence there, consider all of them to be principal performers.

> When only one performer is named in the chief source of information, consider that performer to be a principal performer.

> When no performers are named in the chief source of information, consider that there are no principal performers.

> In judging relative prominence on the basis of wording, layout, and typography, consider names printed in the same size and style of lettering in association with one another to have equal prominence. When names appear in the same size and style of lettering but in different areas of the same source of information, consider those in a location implying superiority (e.g., a higher position) to have greater prominence. Do not consider names near the beginning of a list or sequence to have greater prominence than those near the end.

Chief source of information:
> JESS WALTER SINGS
> CLASSIC FOLK SONGS
> Jess Walters, baritone
> Hector Garcia, guitar

Main entry under the heading for Walters as principal performer

Chief source of information:
> Joan Sutherland
> SONGS MY MOTHER TAUGHT ME
> Songs by Dvořák, Mendelssohn, Massenet,
> Gounod, Delibes, Grieg, Liszt,
> and others
> Richard Bonynge
> The New Philharmonia Orchestra

Main entry under the heading for Sutherland as principal performer

Chief source of information:

SONATAS OF J.S. BACH AND SONS
JEAN-PIERRE RAMPAL, Flute
ISAAC STERN, Violin
JOHN STEELE RITTER,
Harpsichord and Fortepiano
LESLIE PARNAS, Cello

Main entry under title: Rampal, Stern, Ritter, and Parnas are principal performers

Chief source of information:

MUSIC OF CHABRIER AND MASSENET
Detroit Symphony Orchestra
Paul Paray

Main entry under the heading for the orchestra
Added entry under the heading for Paray
(The orchestra and Paray are principal performers)

Chief source of information:

LAS VOCES DE LOS CAMPESINOS

Francisco García and Pablo and Juanita Saludado sing *corridos* about the farm workers and their union
Main entry under the heading for García
Added entries under the headings for P. Saludado and J. Saludado
(García and the Saludados are principal performers)

Chief source of information:

SARAH BERNHARDT & THE COQUELIN BROTHERS

(Dramatic readings performed by Sarah Bernhardt, Constant Coquelin, and Ernest Coquelin)
Main entry under the heading for Bernhardt
Added entries under the headings for C. Coquelin and E. Coquelin
(Bernhardt, C. Coquelin, and E. Coquelin are principal performers)

Chief source of information:

SONGS OF THE WOBBLIES
with
Joe Glazer

(Sung by Glazer, with instrumental ensemble)
Main entry under the heading for Glazer as principal performer

Chief source of information:

Serge Cassel
POESIE ET PROSE FRANÇAISES

(Various poems and prose selections read by Serge Cassel)
Main entry under the heading for Cassel as principal performer

Chief source of information:

SOUTHERN CLAWHAMMER BANJO

(No performers named)
Main entry under title
(No principal performers)

(*CSB* 25: 59-61)

21.23D RI See RI 21.23C. (*CSB* 25:62)

COLLECTIVE ACTIVITY OF A CORPORATE BODY

21.1B2(e) One should also remain aware of the provisions of this rule that stipulate main entry under a corporate body for a performing group whose "responsibility goes beyond that of mere performance." (*AACR 2 21.1B2(e)*) While this provision is offered here as justification for main entry under corporate body, it is unlikely that such a body would not also appear as principal performer. It is germane, though, when a performing corporate body has been transcribed in the statement of responsibility, to consider that body's responsibility for creation of the work recorded to supersede that of any composer or author listed. The scope of this provision is further narrowed by the Library of Congress Rule Interpretation:

RI This category emphasizes that the responsibility of a performing group must go beyond "mere performance, execution, etc." This means that the group must be responsible to a major degree for the artistic content of the work being performed. A typical example is an acting group that performs by means of improvisation. The group collectively "plans" the drama, that is, determines the broad outline of the plot, the nature of the characters, etc., in the absence of a written dialogue. The development of the drama proceeds entirely on the basis of improvised dialogue. The performance is recorded and it is the recording that is being cataloged. (*CSB 25:54*)

FORM OF ENTRY

There are no rules for forms of entry specifically for use with music materials. However, because forms of entry are based on the forms found in chief sources of information, there are a few extra considerations.

COMPOSERS

Composers should be treated as authors.

22.1B RI Treat a music composer as an author and determine the name from the form found in the chief source for the published music. If no form in the published music is in the composer's language, determine the name from reference sources of the composer's country of residence or activity. If the name is not listed in these reference sources, use the name found in the published music. (*CSB 26:15*)

PERFORMERS

For performers, apply the second sentence of rule 22.1B and determine the name from reference sources in his or her language, or issued in his or her country of residence or activity. Consider a performer's recordings among the "reference sources."

When a performer is also known as a composer, a determination should be made about whether he or she is known primarily as a composer or as a performer. If the person is primarily known as a performer, establish the name from chief sources of information on recordings. Otherwise, or in the case of doubt, prefer the form found on chief sources of information in the published music.

NAMES NOT CONVEYING THE IDEA OF A CORPORATE BODY

24.4B RI   In dealing with performing groups, apply the following:

1) If the name contains a word that specifically designates a performing group or a corporate body in general (e.g., Band, Consort, Society) or contains a collective or plural noun (e.g., Ramblers, Boys, Hot Seven) do not add a designation to the name;

2) If the name is extremely vague, consisting primarily of single common words (e.g. Circle, Who, Jets) or the name has the appearance of a personal name (e.g., Jethro Tull), add a designation to the name;

3) If the name falls between the above two categories (e.g., Led Zeppelin, Jefferson Airplane, Road Apple, L.A. Contempo), add a designation to the name.

If there is doubt whether a designation should be added, add it.

Use the designation "(Musical group)" unless special circumstances (such as a conflict) require a more specific term. (*MCB* 13:11:2-3)

SERIES ENTERED UNDER TITLE

For series on music or sound recordings apply Library of Congress Rule Interpretation 25.5B (*CSB* 32:34-41). Generally, qualifying terms are added to the uniform title for a series only when the series conflicts with another work with the same title proper. In most cases the place of publication is considered the appropriate addition to a uniform title for a series. (See also SERIES ENTERED UNDER A NAME HEADING below.)

CHAPTER 3: UNIFORM TITLES

INTRODUCTION

Uniform titles will be used for almost all music materials. It is in this aspect of formulating the access point for a description of an item that the distinction between the intellectual entity (the work) and its present physical manifestation (the item that contains it) is not only most pertinent, but also most important.

Due to historical precedents in music and music publishing, it is less likely that the title from the chief source on any item will coincide with that of the original, or even the most widely known, title of the work. Because so-called "generic" titles might contain several elements that can be presented in differing languages, styles, or order from one publication to the next, it is less likely that the title will be constant from one edition to another. Finally, because of the nature of music collections, the typical disc or score is more likely to represent another manifestation of a particular work than it is to contain a new work altogether.

By virtue of all these reasons, at least one or more of the typical functions for uniform titles is likely to come into play for any musical works cataloged. These functions are:

1) to draw together in the catalog bibliographic descriptions of various physical manifestations of a particular work;

2) to identify a work when the title by which the work is commonly known differs from the title given on the item that contains it;

3) to distinguish different works that have similar or like titles; and,

4) to draw together in the catalog bibliographic descriptions of items that contain like types of works (i.e. all collective uniform titles). (Cf. *AACR 2* 25.1)

Application at the Library of Congress is determined as follows:

25.25 MCD   When the uniform title assigned to a particular manifestation of a musical work is identical (except for the deletion of an initial article) to the title proper of the item (for collections without a collective title, see RI 21.30J(2) [cf. *CSB* 18:38] for guidance as to what constitutes the title proper), do not include the uniform title in the bibliographic record for the item ... unless one or more of the following exceptions applies:

> 1) If the uniform title contains any of the elements prescribed as additions in 25.29-25.31, include the uniform title in the bibliographic record.

> 2) If the uniform title is for one or more parts of a musical work (25.32), include it in the bibliographic record.

3) If the uniform title is a collective one (25.34-25.36), include it in the bibliographic record.

4) If a uniform title must be formulated for a work in order to delete an alternative title (RI 25.3B(1) [cf. *CSB* 13:44]), add the uniform title to the bibliographic records for all manifestations of thework.

5) If a uniform title is required for a work entered under title and a qualifier must be added to the uniform title to distinguish the work from others with the same title, include the uniform title in the bibliographic records for all manifestations of the work (RI 25.5B(6) [unpublished RI]). (*MCB* 13:1:5)

The "title proper" for an item without a collective title is defined as all the data recorded up to the first recorded other title information (including parallel title) or the first statement of responsibility, whichever comes first. (*MCB* 14:6:2)

This decision requires the cataloger to know (or at least to have an educated idea about) the form a uniform title for a musical work would take if it were assigned. Thus the uniform title should be formulated whether it is to be applied or not.

Whatever the rationale, the formulation of a uniform title can seem puzzling to the uninitiated. Rules governing *all* uniform titles are contained in *AACR 2* chapter 25. Rules that are music-specific appear in rules 25.25-25.36. General instruction on which rules to apply is contained in rule 25.25:

25.25 Formulate a uniform title for a musical work as instructed in 25.26-25.36. Use the general rules 25.1-25.7 insofar as they apply to music and are not contradicted by the following rules (25.26-25.36). (*AACR 2* p. 473)

While the specific formulation of any uniform title is a unique process that blends elements of research, precedent, and interpretation, the following general pattern is always applicable and will govern the specific discussion that follows.

1) Choose the title of the work in the original language (the initial title element).
2) Manipulate the initial title element (i.e., drop superfluous words, pluralize and/or render into English, etc.).
3) If the initial title element is "generic," make additions to it to make it distinctive or unique.
4) Add further identifying elements to the formulated uniform title (whether its origin is distinctive or generic) to resolve conflicts among different works with like uniform titles.
5) If the work represented is an excerpt, add a designation to represent the part of the work.
6) Add terms that indicate the manifestation in hand.

SELECTION OF TITLES

The first step in the formulation of a uniform title is the selection of the initial title element. What really must be done at this stage is to identify the work(s) contained in the item being cataloged, then to select the version of the title for that work. This is the initial title element which will then be used to formulate the uniform title. The application of rule 25.26B is a key factor at this point. Bear in mind that a work might meet one or all of the conditions outlined there.

Here, with examples inserted, are those conditions:

25.26B 1) a work that is a single unit intended for performance as a whole:

Suite for 8 violas

Pictures from an exhibition
Die Entführung aus dem Serail
String quartet
Symphonie Nr. 40
Carnaval op. 9
Concerto in A minor, op.54
Die Zauberflöte
War requiem

2) a set of works with a group title (not necessarily intended for performance as a whole):

Madrigali guerrieri et amoroso, 8. livre
Sonaten für Klavier und Violine
12 light duos for two flutes

3) a group of works with a single opus number:

15 solos for a German flute, oboe, or violin and continuo, op.1
Die frühen Streichquartette, op. 18

(*AACR* 2 p. 474)

The point of this rule is to illustrate the broadest possible definition of "work." In fact, most musical materials contain either a work (from whatever category) or an excerpt from a work. In either case the work might appear in a somewhat altered version. If the alteration is by the original composer, apply the following Music Cataloging Decision:

MCD   If a composer changes the title and/or assigns a new opus number for his revised, transcribed, recomposed, reordered, altered, arranged, or adapted version of an earlier work, treat this new version as another work, not as part of, or as an arrangement of, the earlier work.

```
Stravinsky, Igor
   Les cinq doigts : 8 pièces très faciles sur 5 notes, pour piano
...

Stravinsky, Igor
   [Instrumental miniatures]
   Eight instrumental miniatures ...
```
(Recomposed in 1962 for 15 winds and strings)

```
Prokofiev, Sergey
   [Romeo i Dzhul´etta (Ballet)]
   Romeo and Juliet : complete ballet, op.64 ...

Prokofiev, Sergey
   [Romeo i Dzhul´etta (Piano work)]
   Romeo i Dzhul´etta : desiat´ p´es dlia fortepiano, op. 75 ...
```

If the new version's title has not been changed and identifying elements (such as opus numbers) unique to the new version are lacking, yet the revision and/or addition of new material by the composer is extensive, treat the new version as another work.

```
Hindemith, Paul
   [Marienleben (1923)]
   Das Marienleben : (original version) ...
```

```
Hindemith, Paul
   [Marienleben (1948)]
   Das Marienleben ...
   ("Neue Fassung (1948) der Original-Ausgabe, Opus 27 (1922-
1923)")
```

If the revised version or edition of a composer's work retains the same title and opus number as the original version, and the revision is one of different instrumentation within the same broad medium (e.g., orchestra, instrumental ensemble, band) rather than extensive overall revision and the introduction of new material, use the uniform title for the original and revised version.

```
Schoenberg, Arnold
   [Stücke, orchestra, op. 16]
   Fünf Orchesterstücke, op. 16 : Original-fassung ...

Schoenberg, Arnold
   [Stücke, orchestra, op. 16]
   Five pieces for orchestra, op. 16 : new version = Fünf
Orchesterstücke ...
   ("Revised edition, reduced for normal-sized orchestra by the
composer")

Stravinsky, Igor
   Petrushka : complete original 1911 version ...

Stravinsky, Igor
   [Petrushka]
   Petrouchka : burleske in four scenes (revised 1947 version)
...
```

(*MCB* 13:9:1-3)

25.27A Next is the choice among different language forms of the initial title element. In following the concept of entry under the heading most likely to be sought and/or commonly identified by the user, rule 25.27A specifies use of "the composer's original title in the language in which it was formulated ... [unless] a later title in the same language is better known ..." (*AACR* 2 p. 474)

The parenthetical reference in rule 25.27A to the basic rules (25.1-25.4) provides options in case of doubt. The Library of Congress Music Cataloging Decision offers a clearer fallback:

MCD   If the title of the first edition of a work is not known to be different in wording or language from the composer's original title, use the first edition title as the basis for the uniform title unless a later title in the same language is better known. (*MCB* 12:12:5)

Because the formulation of a uniform title is another step in the formulation of an authority-controlled access point, it is logical to assume that the initial formulation of a uniform title might require significant research on the part of the cataloger. The experienced music cataloger will, of course, garner clues from the form, style/period of composition, knowledge of other works by the same composer or by others of the composer's contemporaries, the reputation of a particular publisher, etc. These clues will help shorten the amount of time spent searching in reference sources. Nevertheless, there are a few shortcuts.

Ideally, each title should be verified in a biobibliographical source (for a list of sources see Chapter 6). Usually a thematic index is the best place to verify the composer's original title, as well as the title of the first edition, and to determine the language in which they were formulated. It is also helpful for determining in one step the title of a whole work and of all of its parts, should the work in question actually constitute an excerpt.

Once the language is determined, standard music encyclopedias in that language can be checked to determine whether a later, better-known title in the original language should be preferred. Ideally at least three modern sources should be checked to determine whether a particular form of title is really better known (the sources should all agree).

Practically speaking, there are shortcuts that can reduce much of this work. The practicality of any particular approach depends to a large degree upon the particulars of the work being verified, but the following are general guidelines:

1) Works composed to about 1800, and works by prolific composers, should be verified first in thematic indexes and then in encyclopedias that include lists of works.

2) Works composed after 1800 can be dealt with more efficiently by first checking standard encyclopedias in the composer's language. In the event that a later, better-known title exists, it will be found in this manner, regardless of the composer's original title.

3) A recently composed work might exist in no other manifestation than that in hand, so one can use the titles as they appear on the item as long as they appear to be formulated in the composer's language or in the language of the country of his or her principal residence or activity.

In each case, the amount of verification required will depend upon the results of the initial check. If the title in hand is the same as that in a standard list, less verification will be necessary than is the case when inconsistency results. In all cases the cataloger should remain aware of the dual functions the uniform title will serve, identification and differentiation. During the verification process one must check not only for information to identify the work in hand, but also for information about other works by the same composer in the event that distinguishing elements will be required.

Note that rule 25.27.C provides special treatment for works that have titles based upon the name of a type of composition and that are commonly cited as one of a numbered sequence of works of that particular type of composition.

25.27C MCD The word "titles" in 25.27C means titles arrived at by the application of 25.26A. If a work is cited as one of a numbered sequence of compositions of a particular type but its title does not include the name of the type, 25.27C does not apply.

```
Kelterborn, Rudolf
      Espansioni : Sinfonie III ...
      (Uniform title, Espansioni, not included in bibliographic record;  Cf. MCD 25.25, above)
```

but

```
Hovhaness, Alan
      [Symphonies, no. 21, op. 234]
      Symphony Etchmiadzin : Symphony no. 21 ...
```

Note that the word "cited" in 25.27C means that the work in question must be explicitly identified as one of a numbered sequence of compositions in at least one reference source or manifestation. (*MCB* 13:1:6)

MANIPULATION OF THE INITIAL TITLE ELEMENT

Once an initial title element has been chosen, it must be manipulated to make it "uniform." The first step is to apply the list at rule 25.26A to strip away excess words. This is very much the same decision-making process that was encountered earlier in formulating the description. If the remaining title element is distinctive, it will be used virtually unaltered.

The Library of Congress also deletes initial articles.

25.3A/25.4A RI If a uniform title begins with an article (definite or indefinite) and is in the nominative case (for inflected languages), delete the article in all cases, even when the uniform title is entered under a name ...

```
                    Verdi, Giuseppe
                        [Trovatore.  Balen del suo sorriso]
```

not

```
                    Verdi, Giuseppe
                        [Il Trovatore.  Il balen del suo sorriso]
```

(*CSB* 11: 45-46)

25.3B RI   If the title proper of a work includes an alternative title, and a uniform title is needed for the work (e.g., the item being cataloged is a translation or the work is used in a subject or added entry), omit the alternative title from the uniform title. This same uniform title is used in all entries for the work. (*CSB* 13:44)

25.26A MCD Normally consider phrases such as "a due," "a cinque," etc., to be statements of medium of performance and not part of the title as defined in this rule.

For works with titles such as *quartetto concertante*, *duo concertant*, etc. (but not *sinfonia concertante* -- see 25.27B), normally consider the word "concertante" or its equivalent to be an adjective or epithet not part of the original title of the work, and omit it from the uniform title.

```
                    Vanhal, Johann Baptist
                        [Quartets, flute, violin, viola, violoncello, op. 14]
                        Sei quartetti concertantte : a flauto o violino, violino, alto
                    e basso, op. 14 ...

                        [Quartets, strings, op. 1]
                        Six quatuors concertantes : à 2 violons, alto et basse,
                    oeuvre 1 ...

                        [Quartets, strings, op. 13]
                        Sei quartetti a due violini, alto et basso, opera 13a ...
```

(*MCB* 13:6:2)

No further manipulation of the title element takes place in distinctive uniform titles, unless required to resolve conflicts.

Other initial title elements (referred to as "generic") fall into two categories:

1) titles consisting solely of the name of one type of composition (Quartet, Symphonie, Concerto, Requiem); or,

2) titles consisting of more than one name of one type of composition (Prelude and fugue, Introduction and allegro, Rondo with fugato).

25.27B MCD Consider commonly used liturgical titles such as Requiem, Te Deum, Salve Regina, Dixit Dominus, etc., to be generic terms. If a plural form is required, form one if possible by adding the letter *s* to the last word of the title; if this is not convenient, consider the plural to be the same as the singular. Apply 25.29A2(a) and do not normally include a statement of medium of performance. (*MCB* 12:7:2)

Titles that fall into the first category must be regularized and given in English if the name is the same or cognate in English, French, German, and Italian. If the composer wrote more than one work of the type, the term is given in the plural form.

MCD   When cataloging the first occurrence of a work of a particular type by a composer:

a) If the composer is deceased, search reference sources to determine whether the composer wrote more than one work of the type, and use singular or plural according to the information found.

b) If the composer is living, use the singular in the uniform title unless the work being cataloged bears a serial number (including 1); in that case use the plural on the assumption that the composer has written or intends to write more works of the type. (*MCB* 12:6:3)

Exceptions are made for the following terms:

> étude
> fantasia   } not rendered into English
> Sinfonia concertante
>
> duo, duet, etc.   } always use *duet*
>
> Sonata a tre, etc.   } always use Trio sonatas

For the terms "Melodie," "Melodies," "Melody," etc., the Library of Congress applies the following Music Cataloging Decision:

25.27B MCD   When a French work for solo voice and keyboard stringed instrument has the title *Mélodie* or *Mélodies*, do not translate the title into English, since the cognate words in English and other languages do not have the specific meaning of the French word. Consider the medium of performance to be implied by the title and do not include it in the uniform title (25.29A2(a)).

When a French work for solo voice and accompaniment of other than a keyboard stringed instrument alone, or without accompaniment, has *Mélodie* or *Mélodies*, do not translate the title into English. Include the medium of accompaniment or a statement of the absence of accompaniment. (25.29H3).

When the word *Mélody* or *Mélodies* or its cognate in another language (including French) is the title of any other work, consider it the name of a type of composition. Use the English form in the uniform titles and include the medium of performance (25.29A1). (*MCB* 12:10:3)

Titles that fall into the second category (i.e., those consisting of the names of two or more types of composition) are used unaltered.

```
Introduction und Allegro appassionato
Preludium und Fuge
Variationen und Fuge über ein Originalthema
```

ADDITIONS TO THE INITIAL TITLE ELEMENT

25.29-25.32   Initial title elements that consist of the unmodified name(s) of a type or types of composition are likely to conflict in an author file unless distinguishing elements are added. Those elements specified by *AACR 2* are: 1) the medium of performance; 2) serial, opus, or thematic index numbering; 3) key or tonal center; and, when all else fails to produce a unique uniform title, 4) date of composition or original publication, or place of composition, or name of first publisher. This fourth category is used only rarely.

MEDIUM OF PERFORMANCE

25.29A Rule 25.29A governs the conditions under which medium of performance may be added to the title element. The four instances in which medium of performance should not be added are listed in rule 25.29A2.

The first instance is titles that consist of names of types of composition that imply a medium of performance. "Chorale prelude" (organ is implied) and "overture and symphony" (orchestra is implied) are the most obvious examples listed in *AACR 2*. In case of doubt the cataloger should check a standard reference source for a definition of the type of composition. For instance, *Chorale prelude* is usually defined as "*an organ composition* based on a Protestant chorale." (*Harvard Dictionary of Music*, p. 160. Emphasis added)

This criterion works both ways. That is, in cases where the work in question is composed for a medium of performance *other than that implied by its title*, a statement of medium of performance *is* added to the uniform title.

```
[Symphonies, organ ...]
[Symphonies, band ...]
[Symphonies, string orchestra ...]
```

The second instance is when the work in question is a set of works (e.g., Handel's opus 1, which contains fifteen sonatas for diverse solo instruments) or a series of works (e.g., Monteverdi's madrigal sets, which are numbered serially, but comprise varying performance media) for which there is no single medium of performance.

The third instance is when no medium of performance is designated by the composer.

```
Vinci, Pietro
     [Motetti i ricercari]
     [For 3 voices]
```

The fourth instance is when the medium is judged too complex or not useful in file organization. Mozart's *Divertimenti* are a notorious example and are used as illustrations in *AACR 2*. Because there are so many *Divertimenti* (somewhere between 20 and 30, depending upon the source), all for varying instrumental combinations, the file would be difficult to understand were medium statements added to each. A considerably more convenient arrangement results from using Köchel thematic index numbers:

```
Mozart, Wolfgang Amadeus
     [Divertimenti, K. 131, D major]
     (For orchestra)

     [Divertimenti, K. 136, D major]
     (For string quartet)

     [Divertimenti, K. 137, B major]
     (For string quartet)

     [Divertimenti, K. 186, B major]
     (For wind ensemble)
```

25.29A1 MCD Do not apply this rule to titles consisting of two words each of which alone would be the name of a type of composition, when the combination of the two words produces a distinctive title (cf. RI 25.27B, first paragraph).

```
          [Humoreske-bagateller]
    not   [Humoreske-bagateller, piano ...]
```

(*MCB* 16:9:3)

25.29A1-2 MCD Although 25.29A2(a) seems to prohibit the use of statements of medium of performance in uniform titles whose first element (the "title" as defined in 25.26A) is "Mass" or "Requiem," add the medium of performance to such uniform titles when no other information is available to distinguish between two or more works by the same composer.

```
Byrd, William
    [Masses, voices (3)]

Byrd, William
    [Masses, voices (5)]
```

For the title *Mélody* or *Mélodies* and its cognates in other languages, and for commonly used liturgical titles such as *Requiem*, *Te Deum*, *Salve Regino*, *Dixit Dominus*, etc., see MCD 25.27B, above. (*MCB* 12:10:3)

25.29A3-4 When the medium of performance is stated, generally the statement is limited to three elements, to be listed in a combination of score and featured instrument/accompaniment order. List voices first:

```
[Canons, women's voice, piano ...]
```

List the keyboard instrument first if there are no voices and there is more than one non-keyboard instrument:

```
[Trios, piano, clarinet, violoncello ...]
```

but

```
[Sonatas, violin, piano ...]
```

Other instruments should be listed in score order, rule 25.29A3 specifying "the order of other instruments in score order." (*AACR* 2 p. 478) Traditional practice has been to arrange instruments and/or voices in order of descending pitch within groups:

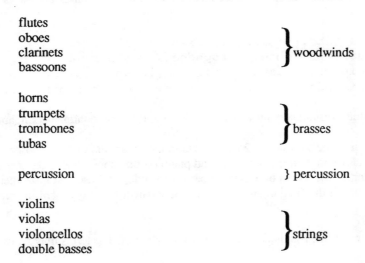

```
flutes
oboes          } woodwinds
clarinets
bassoons

horns
trumpets       } brasses
trombones
tubas

percussion     } percussion

violins
violas         } strings
violoncellos
double basses
```

When cataloging a recording without benefit of a printed score, this traditional order may be used.

When *continuo* is an element of the medium of performance, it is always stated last.

The final condition involves the number of parts for a particular instrument or voice. In general the number is given in parentheses following the name of the instrument or voice, unless the number is implied by other elements of the uniform title (rule 25.29A4).

CONSTRUCTING THE STATEMENT OF MEDIUM

25.29B-J The rules in this section of *AACR 2* are sufficiently explicit. General advice about constructing a statement of medium of performance would include an admonition that the segments of rule 25.29 are not necessarily hierarchical, and that they are in many instances interdependent. For example, the accompanying ensemble required by rule 25.29G might be one of those specified in rule 25.29F or rule 25.29E. There are, however, a number of rule interpretations and/or Music Cataloging Decisions from the Library of Congress that will help elucidate or expand provisions of the various segments. Here, interspersed with a few additional caveats, are those instructions:

25.29C The list in the first paragraph of this rule might better appear in three columns:

ensemble	*instrumentation*	*in uniform title*
string trio	(vln, vla, vlnclo)	[Trios, strings ...]
string quartet	(2 vlns, vla, vlnclo)	[Quartets, strings ...]
woodwind quartet	(fl, ob, cl, bsn)	[Quartets, woodwinds ...]
wind quintet	(fl, ob, cl, hn, bsn)	[Quintets, winds ...]
piano trio	(pno, vln, vlnclo)	[Trios, piano, strings ...]
piano quartet	(pno, vln, vla, vlnclo)	[Quartets, piano, strings ...]
piano quintet	(pno, 2 vlns, vla, vlnclo)	[Quintets, piano, strings ...]

(*AACR 2* p. 479)

If the uniform title begins with the word Trio, Quartet, or Quintet, use the form given in the column on the right.

If the uniform title begins with a name of a type of composition other than Trio, Quartet, or Quintet, use the form in the column on the left.

If the uniform title begins with the word Trio, Quartet, or Quintet, but the instrumentation differs from the seven combinations specified, record the full statement of medium, even if this requires the use of more than three elements:

```
[Quartets, violins, violas, ...]
[Quartets, oboe, saxophones, bassoon ...]
[Quintets, piano, violins, violas ...]
[Quintets, flutes, clarinet, oboe, bassoon ...]
```

25.29D RI Use the following instrument names: violoncello, English horn, contrabassoon, and timpani.

If the application of the subrules of 25.29 results in the separation of a composer's works between harpsichord or clavichord on the one hand and piano on the other, choose the instrument for which the major portion of the works of a given type was intended and use that instrument name for all works of the type. If the "major" instrument is not apparent, use "keyboard instrument." (*CSB* 20:33)

25.29D2 MCD The list of terms in this rule is illustrative, not restrictive. Other terms may be used as necessary.

```
clavichord, 3 hands
harpsichord (3)
player-piano
```

(*MCB* 14:3:1)

25.29D4 Use the term "continuo" whether the bass line is figured or not.

25.29E RI   In the list of terms for groups of instruments, use "plucked instruments" instead of "plectral instruments."

Use the phrase "instrumental ensemble" as a statement of medium that is added to a title in a uniform title only if the medium is a group of diverse instruments not already provided for by other terms in the list.

(*CSB* 14:55)

In dealing with ensembles of wind instruments, the Library of Congress Music Cataloging Decision instructs:

MCD   Use "winds" in uniform titles for chamber music combinations only when it is either not possible (e.g. because of the three-element limitation in 25.29A3) or not more informative to use "woodwinds" or "brasses" together with the names of individual instruments. Specifically:

a) For works for two different woodwind instruments and two different brass instruments, state the medium of performance simply as "winds." Do not list the woodwind instruments individually and group the woodwind instruments (e.g., "flute, oboe, brasses") or group the woodwind instruments and list the brass instruments individually (e.g., "woodwinds, trumpets (2), horn") since the choice of which to list and which to group is arbitrary; do not use "woodwinds, brasses," since this would convey no additional information.

b) For works for two different woodwind instruments and three or more different brass instruments or for two different brass instruments and three or more different woodwind instruments, list the two and group the others,

```
[Serenade, woodwinds, horn, trombone ...]
[Suite, flutes (2), oboe, brasses ...]
```

c) For works for three or more different brass instruments and three or more different woodwind instruments, use "winds," not "woodwinds, brasses."

d) For works for two or more different woodwind instruments, two or more different brass instruments, and one other instrument or group of instruments, use "winds," not "woodwinds, brasses."

```
[Suite, piano, winds]
```
(*For piano, flute, oboe, trumpet, and trombone*)

Note that in uniform titles beginning with the word "Trio(s)," "Quartet(s)," or "Quintet(s)," the instruments must always be listed individually unless the ensemble is a standard combination (25.29C, third paragraph). (*MCB* 13:1:6)

25.29G RI   For an accompanying ensemble that has only one performer to a part, use an appropriate phrase for the group of instruments (e.g., "string ensemble," "wind ensemble," "instrumental ensemble") as a statement of medium that follows the statement for solo instruments in a uniform title. (*CSB* 11:53)

25.29G MCD   The phrase "jazz ensemble" may be used, when appropriate, for either the accompanying ensemble or the group of solo instruments.

```
[Concertos, violin, jazz ensemble ...]
[Concertos, jazz ensemble, orchestra ...]
```

(*MCB* 14:6:3)

25.29H3 Note that the initial title element of the uniform title must be "Songs," "Lieder," "Chansons," etc., *and* the work must *not* be in a popular idiom, before this rule applies. This rule is not applicable to collective uniform titles formulated under rule 25.36B. While it is extremely unlikely that any work in the popular idiom would be titled "Song," or "Lieder," should this occur, the provisions of this rule do not apply.

OTHER IDENTIFYING ELEMENTS

25.31 The serial number, opus number, and key should be added to titles consisting of the unmodified name(s) of a type or types of composition, following the statement of medium of performance (if any). In the absence of a serial and/or opus number, or in certain cases in preference to them, a thematic index number is used.

25.31A1 RI   When adding a serial number, opus or thematic index number, or key to a title that consists solely of the name(s) of type(s) of composition or to a title that conflicts, generally use English terms and arabic numbers. Abbreviate both English and non-English terms and arabic numbers. Abbreviate both English and non-English terms in accord with Appendix B and transcribe numbers in accord with Appendix C. (*CSB* 11:53)

Do not confuse the instruction in rule 25.31A3 to include "any number within the opus" with the somewhat different provisons for excerpts. This instruction is intended to apply to individually published works that are serially numbered sequentially, but that also bear inclusive opus numbering. Such cases are rare.

AUTHORIZED THEMATIC INDEXES

25.31A4 The following list, updated regularly in *Music Cataloging Bulletin*, comprises those "certain composers" referred to in rule 25.31A4 for whom thematic index numbers are to be preferred. (For complete citations see Chapter 6.)

Composer	Abbrev.	Compiler, etc.
Albinoni, Tomaso	G.	Giazotto
Bach, Carl Philipp Emanuel	W.	Wotquenne
Bach, Johann Christoph Friedrich	W.	Wohlfarth
Bach, Johann Sebastian	BWV	Schmieder
Bach, Wilhelm Friedemann	F.	Falck
Beethoven, Ludwig van	WoO	Kinsky*
Benda, Franz	L.	Lee
Boccherini, Luigi	G.	Gerard
Bull, John	MB	Musica Brittanica**
Buxtehude, Dietrich	BuxWv	Karstadt
Charpentier, Marc Antoine	H.	Hitchcock***
Clementi, Muzio	T.	Tyson****
Coperario, John	RC	Charteris
Eybler, Joseph, Edler von	H.	Herrmann
Frederick II, King of Prussia	S.	Spitta
Gabrieli, Giovanni	K.	Kenton
García, Jose Mauricio Nunes	M.	Mattos
Gassmann, Florian Leopold	H.	Hill
Griffes, Charles Tomlinson	A.	Anderson*

Composer	Abbrev.	Compiler, etc.
Handel, George Frideric	B.	Bell
Haydn, Joseph	H.	Hoboken
Hoffmeister, Franz Anton	H	Hickman
Mozart, Wolfgang Amadeus	K.	Köchel 6****
Novotny, Ferenc	S.	Samorjay
Pleyel, Ignaz	B.	Benton
Purcell, Henry	Z.	Zimmerman
Quantz, Johann Joachim	K.	Kohler in Reilly
Ryba, Jakub Jan	N.	Nemecek
Scarlatti, Domenico	K.	Kirkpatrick
Schubert, Franz	D.	Deutsch
Soler, Antonio	M.	Marvin
Strauss, Richard	AV	Mueller von Asow*
Tartini, Giuseppe	D.	Dounias*****
Torelli, Giuseppe	G.	Giegling
Vivaldi, Antonio	RV	Ryom
Viotti, Giovanni Battista	W.	White******
Vogler, Georg Joseph	S.	Schafhautl
Wagenseil, Georg Christoph	WV	Scholz-Michelitsch
Weiss, Silvius Leopold	K.	Klima*******

----
*Abbreviation used only for works without opus no.
**Volumes 14 and 19 (keyboard music)
***In *New Grove*
****Use boldfaced nos.; or nos. from earliest ed. of Köchel
*****Violin concertos
******Instrumental works
*******Roman numerals translated into Arabic

KEY

25.31A5 Add the key as the last element in the uniform title when the initial title element is the name of one or more types of composition. Give the key in the form of an upper case letter followed by the mode (major or minor).

```
Brahms, Johannes
    [Symphonies, no. 4, op. 98, E minor]
```

For twentieth-century works, include the key or upper case letter designating the tonal center if it has been designated by the composer.

MCD For twentieth-century works, include the key in the uniform title if it is part of the composer's original title (25.27A) or the first-edition title used as a substitute for the composer's original title (MCD 25.27A) (before the deletion of elements such as key under 25.26A). (*MCB* 14:10:4)

```
Hindemith, Paul
    [Symphonies, band, Bᵇ]
```

25.31A6 Occasionally these elements will not be sufficient to distinguish among works with otherwise identical characteristics, or they will be unavailable altogether. In these rare cases, other additions, in the order of preference stated in the rule, may be made.

```
Caix d'Hervelois, Lois de, ca. 1670-1760.
    [Pièces (1708)]
    [Pièces (1731)]
```

As before, the best source for this information is a thematic index or a comprehensive bio-bibliographical dictionary. Notes on such sources used by the Library of Congress will appear in name-authority records. Sometimes the Library of Congress Music Section will issue an "operational decision" in the *Music Cataloging Bulletin* that will more fully explain their sources of information.

RESOLVING DISTINCTIVE TITLE CONFLICTS

25.31B1 Often titles that would otherwise remain unmodified because they do not consist solely of the name(s) of a type of composition will conflict if the composer has used the title more than once for completely different works. Many of J.S. Bach's works bear the same titles, due to various thematic or liturgical relationships. A vogue among twentieth-century composers has been to write a series of compositions that have some loose intellectual relationship to one another and to give them all the same title plus a sequential serial number. When such a conflict occurs, there are three ways to resolve it:

1) add a statement of medium of performance;
2) add a descriptive word or phrase enclosed in parentheses; or,
3) add one of the elements specified in rule 25.31A.

When resolving such a conflict it is necessary to be aware of all compositions with the same title by that composer, because only statements of medium of performance or descriptive phrases (but not both) may be used. Identifying-elements from rule 25.31A are used to resolve conflicts that remain despite the addition of one of the two specified elements.

Debussy's works titled *Images* ... are the first example given in the rule. His *Images pour orchestre* and *Images pour piano* are entirely different works, but when the initial title elements are isolated according to rule 25.26A, "Images" is the resulting uniform title for each work. In this case the additon of the medium of performance is sufficient to distinguish between the two works.

```
[Images, orchestra ...]
[Images, piano ...]
```

Works by twentieth-century composers are treated in a Library of Congress Music Cataloging Decision.

MCD For works with titles not consisting of the name of a type of compositon which have serial numbers associated with them (whether the numbers appear as arabic or roman numerals or spelled out, and whether or not they are preceded by the designation "no." or its equivalent), apply 25.29A2(d) to 25.31B1 and omit the medium of performance when a better file arrangement would result.

```
[Antiphony, no. 2]
Antiphony II : variations on a theme of Cavafy ...
```

When cataloging the first work received in such a sequence, it may, however, be advisable to defer the use of a uniform title until another work in the sequence is received, since it will then be easier to see what numbering pattern is being followed. When the second work is cataloged, the bibliographic record(s) for the first will have to be revised to add the uniform title. (*MCB* 16:12:5)

```
Berio, Luciano
   [Sequenza, no. 6]
   Sequenza VI : for viola ...
```

Luciano Berio has written at least nine works titled *Sequenza*, all of which are sometimes considered elaborations of the first, but which are ultimately different works for different performance media. Arranged by medium of performance, they fall out of order both sequentially and chronologically:

```
Sequenza, flute                    (Sequenza I)
Sequenza, harp                     (Sequenza II)
Sequenza, oboe                     (Sequenza VII)
Sequenza, percussion               (Sequenza VIII)
Sequenza, piano                    (Sequenza IV)
Sequenza, soprano                  (Sequenza III)
Sequenza, trombone                 (Sequenza V)
Sequenza, viola                    (Sequenza VI)
Sequenza, violin                   (Sequenza IX)
```

By adding serial enumeration instead of statements of medium of performance a better file arrangement is achieved:

```
[Sequenza, no. 1]
Sequenza I : für Flote ...

[Sequenza, no. 2]
Sequenza II : für Harfe ...

[Sequenza, no. 3]
Sequenza III : für Frauenstimme ...
```

Note that in order to establish the uniform title for *Sequenza VI* it was necessary to have knowledge of the existence and instrumentation of all the works by Berio with the title *Sequenza*. This is the problem addressed by the Music Cataloging Decision above. However, if the cataloger is working with a network such as OCLC, WLN, or RLIN, it is likely that other works in the sequence will have been entered in the bibliographic data base, thus obviating the need to wait to establish the uniform title. Also, it may be possible to check sources such as catalogs of the publisher of the work being cataloged or, for older works, sources such as Vinton's *Dictionary of Contemporary Music* or Anderson's *Contemporary American Composers*, to ascertain the numbering pattern.

The *Goyescas* by Granados are also different works, but a statement of medium of performance would be too complex for the operatic work, so a distinguishing term is used to resolve the conflict.

```
[Goyescas (Opera)]
[Goyescas (Piano work)]
```

J.S. Bach's works include nine different works with the title *Christ Lag in Todesbanden*. One work is a cantata, three are chorales, and five are chorale preludes. Rule 25.29 rules out statements of medium performance as too complex for the cantata and chorales and not sufficiently distinguishing for the chorale preludes. Descriptive terms are employed initially to resolve the conflict, although even this yields only three unique titles for the nine works. Thematic index numbers are added as the distinguishing element provided in rule 25.31A.

```
[Christ lag in Todesbanden (Cantata), BWV 4]
[Christ lag in Todesbanden (Chorale), BWV 277]
[Christ lag in Todesbanden (Chorale), BWV 278]
[Christ lag in Todesbanden (Chorale), BWV 279]
[Christ lag in Todesbanden (Chorale prelude), BWV 625]
[Christ lag in Todesbanden (Chorale prelude), BWV 695]
[Christ lag in Todesbanden (Chorale prelude), BWV 695a]
[Christ lag in Todesbanden (Chorale prelued), BWV 718]
[Christ lag in Todesbanden (Chorale prelude), BWV Anh. 171]
```

Be careful to apply this provision only to different works. Do not confuse this situation with suites that comprise excerpts from a larger work, variant manifestations (e.g., libretto, vocal score, sketches), or modifications (revisions, adaptations, arrangements).

EXCERPTS

25.32   A separately published, performed, recorded, etc., part of a musical work is entered under the heading for the whole work. This provision is different from that for nonmusical works, which are entered under the name of the part. Uniform titles for excerpts will be common in libraries with large collections of chamber music. If analytical added entries are provided for sound recordings, uniform titles for excerpts will also be necessary. Rule 25.32 provides detailed instructions for establishing the uniform titles for excerpts. Remember that the first step is to identify the larger work from which the excerpt is drawn and establish the complete uniform title for it. Rule 25.32A1 covers situations where excerpts (i.e., all the parts of the entire work that could be excerpted), are numbered, have distinctive titles or unique verbal designations, or both. Rule 25.32A2 covers situations where the parts of a work do not have unique designations. Rule 25.32B1 has instructions for dealing with publications that include several parts of a work. Finally, rule 25.32C is a reminder to make additions to indicate the manifestation of the work according to the provisons of rule 25.31B.

    The exact configuration of the uniform title for an excerpt is dependent upon the nature of the entire original work. The cataloger must know whether all the parts of the original work are numbered, titled, or both, and if they are not numbered whether the titles or verbal designations (such as tempo markings of movements, e.g. Allegro) are unique. Uniform titles for excerpts, therefore, should be established from authoritative editions (e.g., manuscripts, first editions, "Urtext" editions, complete works, etc.). Lacking these sources, thematic indexes or, as a last resort, comprehensive bio-bibliographical dictionaries are sometimes useful. The title and/or numerical designation of the part of the work should be used as it appears in the source. That is, it should not be regularized according to rule 25.27B.

25.32A1 RI When selecting the title of a part of a musical work, follow 25.26A and 25.27A but not 25.27B.

    When the number of a part of a work is used in the uniform title of the part, precede the number by the abbreviation "No." ("No," "Nr.," "N.," etc.) when such an abbreviation, or the corresponding word, appears with the numbers of the parts in the source on which the uniform title is based. Give the abbreviation in the language of the first element of the uniform title.

        Brahms, Johannes
          [Ungarische Tänze. Nr. 5]

(*CSB* 33:49-50)

        Vivaldi, Antonio
          [Estro armonico. N. 8]

        Mendelssohn-Bartholdy, Felix
          [Präludien und Fugen, organ, op. 37. Nr. 1]

        Clementi, Muzio
          [Sonatas, piano, op. 24. No. 2]

    However, when the number of the part is used as an addition for the purpose of distinguishing between two or more parts with the same title (RI 25.32A1, last paragraph), precede it by the English abbreviation "No." in all cases.

        Milan, Luis
          [Maestro. Fantasia del primero tono (No. 1)]

(*MCB* 17:2:3)

MCD   For instructions for the formulation of the references prescribed by this rule, see MCD 26.4A1. (*MCB* 15:10:2)

25.32A2 RI   When the number of the part is used as an addition for the purpose of distinguishing between two or more parts with the same title, precede it by the English abbreviation "No." in all cases. (*CSB* 33:50)

25.32B   Two or more excerpts from a single larger work are entered according to the provisions of rule 25.6B. One caveat is associated with the addition of "Selections" to uniform titles for motion picture sound track recordings:

25.32B1 MCD   When evidence is lacking as to whether an "original cast" recording of a musical comedy or an "original sound track" recording of a motion picture score contains all the music, do not add "Selections" to the uniform title. (*MCB* 16:3:5)

25.32B2   Another caveat is encountered with suites drawn from larger works.

```
Tchaikovsky, Peter Ilich
    [Shchelkunchik.   Suite]
```

Shchelkunchik is the uniform title for the work known in English as *The Nutcracker*. The suite represented by this uniform title comprises excerpts from the ballet *Shchelkunchik*. Do not apply this provision to suites that were originally composed as suites.

```
Tchaikovsky, Peter Ilich
    [Suites, orchestra, no.1, op. 43, D minor]
```

(See also MCD 25.32B1 *Separately Published Parts*, above.)

ADDITIONS THAT INDICATE THE MANIFESTATION OF THE WORK

There are three kinds of additions to uniform titles that can be made to indicate the present physical manifestation of the work. They are: 1) "(Sketches);" 2) "Vocal score" or "Chorus score;" and 3) "Libretto" or "Text."

SKETCHES

25.30
```
Beethoven, Ludwig van
    [Quartets, strings, no. 1-6, op. 18 (Sketches)]

Stravinsky, Igor
    [Vesna svîashchennaîa (Sketches)]
```

   MCD For sketchbooks containing sketches for various compositions or miscellaneous sketches, add *Sketches* in parentheses to the appropriate collective uniform title formulated under 25.35 or 25.36 [below].

```
    [Selections (Sketches)]
```

```
[Instrumental music.  Selections (Sketches)]
[Piano music.  Selections (Sketches)]
[Sonatas, piano.  Selections (Sketches)]
[Symphonies, no. 7-9 (Sketches)]
```

(*MCB* 12:10:3)

VOCAL AND CHORUS SCORES

25.31B3 MCD Note that the rule says that "Vocal score" or "Chorus score" is to be added to the uniform title if the item being cataloged is a vocal score or chorus score, i.e., if it has been described as such in the physical description area (cf. 5.5B1 and the decision on that rule above). Therefore, whenever either of these terms is used in the physical description area to describe the item as a whole, the term must also be included in the uniform title. The use of such terms in uniform titles is no longer limited to "works in the larger vocal forms" as in *AACR 1* 243.

This does not apply if the chorus score or vocal score is part of a set which also contains a full score, parts, etc., since the item being cataloged in such cases cannot be said to "be" a chorus score or vocal score. (*MCB* 12:6:4)

```
    Handel, George Frideric
        [Messiah.  Vocal score ...]

    Bizet, Georges
        [Carmen.  Vocal score ...]
```


LIBRETTOS AND SONG TEXTS

25.31B5
```
            Verdi, Giuseppe
                [Forza del destino.  Libretto ...]

            John, Elton
                [Crocodile rock.  Text ...]
```


ADDITIONS THAT INDICATE MODIFICATION OF A WORK

It can be difficult to determine whether a work that appears to be a new version of another work is in fact a modification of it or an entirely new work. In general, modification must be extensive before the new version can be considered to be an entirely new work. In making such decisions, consult the RI for rule 25.26B above.

ARRANGEMENTS

25.31B2 The glossary of *AACR 2* defines an arrangement as "a musical work, or a portion thereof, rewritten for a medium of performance different from that for which the work was originally intended ..." (*AACR 2* p. 563). This definition should be kept in mind when applying rule 25.31B2. The addition of the abbreviation "arr." to a uniform title is contingent upon the amount of change a work has undergone. Arrangement can be either by the original composer or by another person.

Do not use the abbreviation "arr." to describe a work in a popular idiom that describes itself as an arrangement without evidence that an original fixed instrumentation has undergone considerable revision. It is common in popular music for one person to compose a melody and another person to provide an orchestration or other instrumentation to accompany it. This process is referred to idiomatically as arrangement. The abbreviation "arr." should not be used in the uniform title for such works.

Likewise, when a work is revised by the composer and it does not carry a new title or opus number, it is not considered to be an arrangement because the aural iteration of the intellectual entity has not changed substantially.

MCD   If the composer revises a work, retaining the original title and opus number, and the revision is one of different instrumentation within the same broad medium (e.g., orchestra, instrumental ensemble, band) rather than extensive overall revision and the introduction of new material, do not consider the revised version an arrangement, etc. Use the same uniform title for the original and revised versions.

```
Schoenberg, Arnold
    [Stücke, orchestra, op. 16]
    Fünf Orchesterstücke, op. 16 : Original-fassung ...

Schoenberg, Arnold
    [Stücke, orchestra, op. 16]
    Five pieces for orchestra, op. 16 : new version = Fünf
Orchesterstücke ...
    ("Revised edition, reduced for normal-sized orchestra by the
composer.")

Stravinsky, Igor
    Petrushka : complete original 1911 version ...

Stravinky, Igor
    [Petrushka]
    Petrouchka : burleske in four scenes (revised 1947 version)
...
```

(*MCB* 13:9:3)

ADDED ACCOMPANIMENTS, ETC.

25.31B2 MCD For the purposes of this rule, consider a musical work to which an additional accompaniment or additional parts have been added (21.21) to be an arrangement. In addition to the added entry for the composer of the accompaniment or the additional parts prescribed in 21.21, make an analytical added entry for the original work (without *arr.*) ...

```
Bach, Johann Sebastian
    [Sonaten und Partiten, violin, BWV 1001-1006; arr.]
    Sechs Sonaten für Violine solo / von Joh. Seb. Bach ;
herausgegeben von J. Hellmesberger ; Klavierbegleitung von
Robert Schumann ... [1920?]
(Contains the 3 sonatas and 3 partitas)
```

```
Added entries:        I.   Hellmesberger ...
                      II.  Schumann ...
                      III. Bach ... Sonaten und Partiten,
                           violin, BWV 1001-1006.
                           1920.
```

[Further access is provided by subject headings and classification.]

(*MCB* 14:1:3)

SEPARATELY PUBLISHED PARTS

When one or more instrumental parts for a work or a collection of works by one composer are published separately, do not make an addition to the uniform title to bring this out. Use the same uniform title that would be used for a score or a complete set of parts.

```
Bach, Johann Sebastian
   [Wer mich liebet, der wird mein Wort halten, BWV 74]
   Kantate Nr. 74 : Wer mich liebet, der wird mein Wort halten :
BWV 74 / Joh. Seb. Bach ; Continuo-Aussetzsung von Ulrich
Haverkampf. -- Orgel. -- Wiesbaden : Breitkopf & Härtel,
c1982.
   1 part (32 p.) ...

Bach, Johann Sebastian
   [Vocal music.  Selections]
   The flute solos from the Bach cantatas, passions, and oratorios
...

Strauss, Richard
   [Orchestra music.  Selections]
   Orchesterstudien für Flöte : aus Richard Strauss' symphonischen
Werken ...
```

(*MCB* 16:3:5)

ALTERNATIVE INSTRUMENTS

Do not consider to be an arrangement

1) a work composed before 1800 for a baroque, Renaissance, or other early instrument (viola da gamba, recorder, etc.) which is edited for or performed on a contemporary instrument;

2) a work for a melody instrument which is edited for or performed on an alternative instrument specified by the composer or in early editions, preferably the first

--provided the key is unchanged and the notation has not been significantly changed.

```
Bach, Johann Sebastian
   [Sonatas, viola da gamba, harpsichord, BWV 1027-1029]
   Sonatas for cello and piano, BWV 1027, 1028, 1029 [sound
recording] ...
```

```
Kuhlau, Friedrich
    [Sonatas, violin, piano, op. 79, no.1]
    Sonate en fa majeur pour flute & piano, op. 79, no. 1 ...
    (Originally for violin or flute and piano) ...
```

(*MCB* 17:3:2)

ALTERATIONS OF MUSICO-DRAMATIC WORKS

25.31B4 When the non-musical portions of a dramatic work have been substantially altered or entirely replaced (not including translations, however), *and* the title has changed, the title of the new dramatic work is added in parentheses following the uniform title of the original musical work.

```
Bizet, Georges
    [Carmen (Carmen Jones)]
    Carmen Jones / by Oscar Hammerstein II ...
    (Hammerstein updated the libretto)
```

TRANSLATIONS AND OTHER LANGUAGE EDITIONS

25.31B6-7, 25.5D If the text of a work is a translation, add the language(s) following the title element. Language names are formulated according to a Library of Congress Rule Interpretation.

RI   When naming a language in a uniform title, base the name on the form used in *Library of Congress Subject Headings.* Greek represents a special case. Use "Greek" for classical Greek and modern Greek. If, however, the item is a translation from classical Greek into modern Greek, use "Greek (Modern Greek)" in the uniform title. If the item includes text in both, use "Greek (Modern Greek)" and "Greek (Classical Greek)" in the uniform title. (*CSB* 30:20)

If the text is liturgical, the language is always added, whether or not a translation is present.

COLLECTIONS

There are four categories of collections, each of which receives a slightly different treatment in the application and formulation of uniform titles. While special rules and examples are present in rules 25.35-25.36, these provisions are heavily dependent upon the rules for non-musical materials in rules 25.7-25.10. The four categories are: 1) two works published together; 2) complete works; 3) selections (or incomplete works); 4) works in a single form (either works of various types in one medium, or works in various media but of one type).

25.33, 25.8 Follow the instructions in rule 25.8 for collections that consist of two individual works published together. Make the main entry under the heading for the first work, and make a composer-title analytical added entry under the heading for the second work.

```
Tchaikovsky, Peter Ilich
   [Suites, orchestra, no. 1, op. 43, D minor]
   Two orchestral suites [sound recording] ...
(Added entry under Tchaikovsky, Peter Ilich ... Suites, orchestra,
no. 3, op. 55, G major)


Feldman, Morton
   [Spring of Chosroes]
   Spring of Chosroes / Morton Feldman. Sonata for violin and piano
/ Artur Schnabel [sound recording] ...
(Added entry under Schnabel, Artur ... Sonatas, violin, piano)
```

COLLECTIVE UNIFORM TITLES

COMPLETE WORKS

25.34, 25.8 Follow the instructions in rule 25.8. For a collection that comprises (or purports to comprise) the complete works of a person, including collections that were complete at the time of publication, use "Works."

25.8-25.9 RI The collective uniform title "Works" is used frequently enough to make it advisable to use additions for the purposes of making these collective titles distinct, of insuring that translations file after editions in the original language, and of distinguishing between two or more editions published in the same year. To achieve these objectives, apply the following when using "Works":

1) When an item is first cataloged, add the date of publication of the edition at the end of the uniform title. (If a multipart item is incomplete, give the earliest known date. If an item being added to the set was published earlier than the date given in the uniform title do not change the date in the uniform title until the set is complete.) Give the date in the form it would have in an analytical added entry (cf. RI 21.20M). Add the date in all cases, including translations. When making a reference from the title proper of the item (25.5D2), add the date at the end of the title proper in all cases.

2) If two editions bear the same publication date and it becomes necessary to refer to a particular edition in a secondary entry, add the publisher's name after the publication date in the most succinct but intelligible form. Make this addition to the uniform title of the edition(s) needing to be distinguished for secondary entry ... If different editions are published in the same year by the same publisher, add an appropriate qualification to the publisher's name ... (*CSB* 22:34)

```
Handel, George Frideric
   [Works.  1787]
   The works of Handel ... under the inspection and direction
of Dr. Arnold ...


Sheppard, John
   [Works.  1978]
   Collected works ...
```

COMPOSERS AND WRITERS

25.8 RI   If the person has written both musical and literary works, apply the following:

1) If the person is primarily a composer, use the uniform title "Works"

a) for editions containing the complete musical and literary works

b) for editions containing the complete musical works.

(For collections of the literary works alone, use the uniform title "Literary works." For partial collections of the literary works see RI 25.10 [below].

2) If the person is primarily a writer, use the uniform title "Works"

a) for editions containing the complete literary and musical works

b) for editions containing the complete literary works.

(For collections of the musical works alone, use the uniform title "Musical works." For partial collections of the musical works see RI 25.10 (below). (*CSB* 22:35)

SELECTIONS

25.35 Follow instructions in rule 25.9. Use the collective title "Selections" for collections that consist of three or more selections from the works of one composer, originally composed for various performance media *and* in various types of composition.

RI Do not add a date of publication, etc., to the uniform title "Selections" when this is used for collections of musical works by one composer (unless the uniform title is being used as an analytical added entry (cf. 21.30M).) (*CSB* 13:48)

```
Mingus, Charles
   [Selections]
   Nostalgia in Times Square [sound recording] : the immortal
1959 sessions / Charles Mingus ...

Wagner, Richard
   [Selections]
   Wagner et Toscanini [sound recording] ...
```

WORKS OF ONE TYPE OF COMPOSITION OR FOR ONE MEDIUM OF PERFORMANCE

25.36A If all the works in a collection are by one composer and are composed in one broad medium of performance, use the designation of that medium as the uniform title.

```
[Chamber music]
[Instrumental music]
```

Use "Vocal music" or "Choral music" whether or not the selections are accompanied.

25.36A If all the works in a collection are by one composer and are composed for one specific medium of performance, use the statement of that medium of performance as the uniform title.

```
[String quartet music]
```
(All selections for 2 violins, viola, and violoncello; not all titled String quartet)

```
[Piano music]
```

25.36B If all the works in a collection are by one composer and are made up of one type of composition, use the name of the type of composition as the uniform title. Add a statement of medium of performance (cf. rule 25.29 above) if all the selections are composed for the same medium of performance, unless the medium is implicit (e.g., Operas) (cf. rule 25.29A2).

> [Concertos]
> (*All selections are concertos, for various media*)
>
> [Concertos, piano, orchestra]
> (*All selections are piano concertos*)
>
> [Operas]
>
> [Quartets, strings]
> (*All selections are titled* String quartet *and are for 2 violins, viola, and violoncello*)
>
> [Songs]

25.36B RI   For collections of music by a single composer for various motion pictures, use the uniform title "Motion-picture music" or "Motion-picture music. Selections" (without a statement of medium) instead of such uniform titles as "Orchestra music. Selections." (*CSB* 14:56)

25.36 RI   For collections of vocal works, or texts of vocal works, add "Vocal scores," "Chorus scores," "Librettos," "Texts," and/or name of language to any collective uniform title provided by 25.36A or 25.36B. (Note: Use "Texts" if the collection contains both librettos and other texts set to music.)

> [Operettas. Vocal scores]
> [Operas. Librettos. English & Italian]
> [Masses. Latin]
> [Vocal music. Texts. Polyglot]

(*CSB* 20:34)

COMPOSERS AND WRITERS

25.10 RI   If a person has written both musical and literary works, apply the following:

1) If the person is primarily a composer, use the uniform title "Literary works" for editions containing the complete literary works. (For collections containing the complete musical and literary works, apply RI 25.8.) For partial collections of the literary works containing more than one particular form, use the uniform title "Literary works. Selections," *not* "Selections."

2) If the person is primarily a writer, use the uniform title "Musical works" for editions containing the complete musical works. (For collections containing the complete literary and musical works, apply RI 25.8.) For partial collections of the musical works containing various types of compositions in one broad or specific medium or containing one type, use one of the uniform titles specified in 25.36. For partial collections of the musical works containing various types of compositions in various media, use the uniform title "Musical works. Selections," *not* "Selections." (*CSB* 30:21)

SELECTIONS

25.36C For incomplete collections with collective uniform titles add "Selections" to the uniform title.

> **RI**   If the term "Selections" is added to the uniform titles, add it as the last element.
>
> > [Songs. English & German. Selections]
> > [Operas. Librettos. English & Italian. Selections]
> > [Vocal music. Texts. Polyglot. Selections]

```
[Masses.  Latin.  Selections]
[Operettas.  Vocal scores.  Selections]
```

(*CSB* 20:35)

If the selections are a consecutively numbered group, use the inclusive numbering instead of the term "Selections."

```
Tchaikovsky, Peter Ilich
    [Symphonies, no. 1-3]
    The early Tchaikovsky symphonies [sound recording] ...
```

SEPARATELY PUBLISHED PARTS

25.34-25.36 MCD When one or more instrumental parts for a collection of works by one composer are published separately, follow the instructions in MCD 25.31B2. (*MCB* 16:3:5)

ARRANGEMENTS

25.34 Add "arr." to any collective uniform title if the works contained in the collection have undergone arrangement (cf. rule 25.31B2)

```
Bach, Johann Sebastian
    [Selections; arr.]
    Brandenburg boogie [sound recording] / J.S. Bach ; arr. Laurie
Holloway ...

Satie, Erik
    [Piano music.  Selections; arr.]
    Transcriptions for guitar [sound recording] / Satie ...

Williams, John
    [Motion-picture music.  Selections; arr.]
    Pops in space [sound recording] / John Williams ...
```

WORKS WITH THE SAME TITLE THAT IS NOT THE NAME OF A TYPE OF COMPOSITION

25.35-25.36 MCD If all the works in a collection entered under a personal name heading have the same title and this title is not the name of a type of composition, assign a collective uniform title according to 25.35, 25.36A, or 25.36B, using the most specific uniform title that will cover all the works in the collection. If appropriate, add *Selections* according to the first paragraph of 25.36C.

```
[Selections]
(Contains Antiphony I for unaccompanied chorus, Antiphony II
for piano, and Antiphony V for orchestra)

[Instrumental music.  Selections]
(Contains Antiphony III for piano, Antiphony V for orchestra,
and Antiphony VII for string quartet)

[String quartet music]
(Contains Antiphony VII, Antiphony IX, and Antiphony XI, all for
string quartet and the composer's only works in that medium)
```

If, however, the works are consecutively numbered, apply the second paragraph of 25.36C, adding the consecutive numbering to the title of the individual works (in the singular). Do this even if the collection contains all of the composer's works with that title.

```
[Antiphony, no. 2-4]

[Kammermusik, no. 1-7]
```

(*MCB* 12:10:3-4)

SERIES ENTERED UNDER A NAME HEADING

Most series of this type are multipart collections entered under the heading for the composer, and an appropriate uniform title should be assigned according to the provisions of 25.35-25.36. Because these series uniform titles will almost always conflict with the collective uniform titles assigned to monographic publications that are collections, qualifiers must be added. The cataloger first applies RI 25.5B ("Serials/Including Series," *CSB* 32:34-41) and is instructed to add a qualifying term that will distinguish the work. Such qualifiers are created according to the provisions of RI 25.8-25.11 ("Collective Uniform Titles," *CSB* 16:49-50.). When the collective uniform title is "Works," a date is always chosen as the qualifying term. In other cases, RI 25.5B suggests the title proper as the element most likely to provide a unique heading, though the cataloger is allowed leeway in providing a qualifier. A thorough discussion of techniques that have been used by the Library of Congress appears in Richard H. Hunter's article "Uniform Titles for Series: A Summary of Library of Congress Practice as it Relates to Music" (*MCB* 15:12:1-5).

CHAPTER 4: ADDED ENTRIES, INCLUDING ANALYTICS
REFERENCES

ADDED ENTRIES

In general the rules in chapters 21 and 25 specify added entries as required. Further, the cataloger of music materials should exercise judgment in applying rule 21.29B, which provides guidance for making added entries under additional headings the cataloger thinks users might seek.

ORDER OF ADDED ENTRIES

21.29 RI   Give added entries in the following order:

1) Personal name;
2) Personal name/title;
3) Corporate name;
4) Corporate name/title;
5) Uniform title (all instances of works entered under title);
6) Title traced as Title-period;
7) Title traced as Title-colon, followed by a title;
8) Series.

For arrangement within any one of these groupings, generally follow the order in which the justifying data appears in the bibliographic description. If such a criterion is not applicable, use judgment. (*CSB* 12:24)

The rule interpretations and cataloging decisions that follow in this section outline the Library of Congress policy in three particularly complex areas. First are special rules for added entries that might be required in cataloging sound recordings (performers, joint composer, etc.); second are the LC policy decisions on analytical added entries for collections, both printed and recorded; and third are the LC policies on added entries for musical titles.

SPECIAL PROVISIONS FOR SOUND RECORDINGS

JOINT AUTHOR, ARRANGER, LIBRETTIST, ETC.

21.23A-B RI For a sound recording covered by 21.23A or 21.23B, make whatever added entries are prescribed by the rules under which the choice of main entry for the work or works recorded was made (e.g., for a joint author or composer under 21.6C1; for an arranger under 21.18B; for a librettist under 21.19A) as well as any others provided for under RI 21.29.

> *Chief source of information*:
>
>
>
> L'ELISIR D'AMORE -- Highlights
> (Donizetti; Romani)
>
>
>
> (*Music by Donizetti; libretto by Romani, based on Le philtre by Eugene Scribe*)
>
> Main entry under the heading for Donizetti as composer (21.23A, 21.29A); added entries under the headings for Romani and for Scribe's *Le philtre* (21.19A). (*CSB* 25:57)

PERFORMERS NAMED ON A SOUND RECORDING

21.29D RI Make added entries for all performers named on a sound recording (persons or corporate bodies) with the following exceptions:

1) Do not make an added entry for a person who functions entirely or primarily on the item being cataloged as a member of a corporate body for which an added entry is made. Do not consider a conductor or accompanist to be a member of the body he or she conducts or accompanies. If a person's name appears in conjunction with the name of a group, determine whether the corporate name includes this personal name. If the conclusion is that the corporate name does not include the person's name, do not consider the person a member of the group; if the conclusion is that it does include the person's name, consider the person to be a member of the group.

2) If both the chorus and the orchestra of an opera company, opera house, etc., participate in a performance and both are named, along with the name of the parent body, make only a single added entry under the heading for the parent body.

> *On recording*: Bolshoi Theater Orchestra and Chorus
> *(Added entry under the heading for the theater)*

3) When a featured performer is accompanied by an unnamed group that, if it had a name, would be given an added entry as a corporate body, do not make added entries for the individual members of the group. Do not, however, apply this exception to jazz ensembles, even if one or more of the performers is given greater prominence than the others, i.e., normally make added entries for all the individual performers (except any who are covered by exceptions 4) and 5)[below] in such cases.

4) Do not make an added entry for a performer who participates in only a small number of the works in a collection or for a performer whose role is minor (e.g., an announcer on a radio program).

5) Do not make an added entry for a performer who receives main entry heading as principal performer under 21.23C.

6) If there are many performers performing the same function (e.g., singers in an opera), make added entries only for those who are given the greatest prominence in the chief source of information. If all are given equal prominence, make added entries only for those who are given prominence over the

others in other places on the sound recording (e.g., the container, the program booklet, etc.) or, if that criterion does not apply, for those performing the most important functions (e.g., singing the principal roles, acting the principal parts).

Chief source of information (labels):

L'ELISIR D'AMORE -- Highlights
(Donizetti; Romani)
Spiro Malas, Maria Casula, Joan Sutherland,
Luciano Pavarotti, Dominic Cossa
with the Ambrosian Opera Chorus
and the English Chamber Orchestra
conducted by Richard Bonynge

Container:

Donizetti
L'ELISIR D'AMORE Highlights
JOAN SUTHERLAND, LUCIANO PAVAROTTI
Dominic Cossa, Spiro Malas, Maria Casula
Ambrosian Opera Chorus, English Chamber Orchestra
RICHARD BONYNGE

Added entries under the headings for Sutherland, Pavarotti, Bonynge, the chorus, and the orchestra, but not under the heading for Cossa, Malas, or Casula.

If a composer is the main entry heading for a musical work and performs his or her own work(s), make an added entry to represent the performing function. If, however, the composer is represented not by the main entry heading but by a name-title added entry heading, then do not make the added entry to represent the performing function. (*CSB* 34:29-30)

21.30E RI If an added entry is needed on a sound recording for both the chorus and orchestra of an opera company, opera house, etc., make the added entry for the parent body alone. If an added entry is needed for the chorus alone or for the orchestra alone, make the added entry specifically for the body involved. (*CSB* 13:26)

ANALYTICAL ADDED ENTRIES FOR COLLECTIONS

Analytical added entries in the form name-title are made by many libraries for all works contained in sound recording anthologies. For most of them this is the only way to achieve full indexing of musical recordings, because most recordings are by nature anthologies and the main entry heading is rarely sufficient to supply access to more than one work or, in some cases, to a collective uniform title such as *Selections: arr.* The following LC policies apply to both printed music and sound recordings, unless otherwise stated.

COLLECTIONS WITH COLLECTIVE TITLE

21.7B RI *Works that are not collections*

If a work covered by 21.7A is not a collection, make an added entry for each contributor if it contains contributions by no more than three contributors. If such a work contains contributions by four or more contributors, make an added entry for the contributor named first in the chief source. Generally do not make analytical added entries for any of the individual contributions in a work that is not a collection.

Collections

If a collection covered by 21.7A contains no more than three independent works, make an analytical added entry for each work (cf. RI 21.30M [*CSB* 20:12]).

If a collection contains four or more independent works that are entered under no more than three different headings, apply the following:

1) If one heading is represented by one work, make an analytical added entry for the work.

2) If one heading is represented by one excerpt from one work, make an analytical added entry for it.

3) If one heading is represented by two or more consecutively numbered excerpts from one work, make one analytical added entry (25.6B1).

4) If one heading is represented by two unnumbered or nonconsecutively numbered excerpts from one work, make an analytical added entry for each excerpt (25.6B2).

5) If one heading is represented by three or more unnumbered or nonconsecutively numbered excerpts from one work, make one analytical added entry (25.6B3).

6) If one name heading is represented by two works, make an added entry for the name heading alone.

7) If one personal name heading is represented by two works, make an added entry for the name heading alone.

8) If one corporate name heading is represented by three or more works, make an added entry for the name heading alone.

If a collection contains four or more independent works that are entered under four or more different headings, make an added entry for the contributor named first in the chief source.

Sound recordings

If a sound recording collection contains twenty-five or fewer musical works entered under two or more different headings, normally make up to fifteen entries according to the following instructions:

1) If one heading is represented by one work, make an analytical added entry for the work.

2) If one heading is represented by one excerpt from one work, make an analytical added entry for it (25.32A).

3) If one heading is represented by two unnumbered or nonconsecutively numbered excerpts from one work, make one analytical added entry (25.32 B).

4) If one heading is represented by two unnumbered or nonconsecutively numbered excerpts from one work, make an analytical added entry for each excerpt (25.32B).

5) If one heading is represented by three or more unnumbered or nonconsecutively numbered excerpts from one work, make one analytical added entry (25.32B).

6) If one name heading is represented by two works, make an analytical added entry for each work (25.33).

7) If one personal name heading is represented by three or more works, make an analytical added entry using an appropriate collective uniform title (e.g., "Selections," "Piano music. Selections") (25.34-25.36).

Do not make any analytical added entries for sound recording collections

1) containing twenty-five or fewer works that would require more than fifteen analytical added entries

2) containing pop, folk, ethnic, or jazz music

3) containing recitals with an orientation towards performer(s) or instrument(s) rather than musical repertoire

4) that are multipart items but incomplete at the time the collection is cataloged. (*CSB* 28:13-14)

COLLECTIONS WITHOUT COLLECTIVE TITLE

21.7C RI   *Works That Are Not Collections*

If a work covered by 21.7A is not a collection, enter the work under the heading appropriate to the first contribution. If there are three contributors, make added entries for those not chosen for the main entry heading. If there are four or more contributors, do not make added entries for those not chosen for the main entry heading. Generally do not make analytical added entries for the individual contributions in a 21.7A work that is not a collection.

Collections

If a collection covered by 21.7A contains no more than three independent works, enter under the heading appropriate to the first and make analytical added entries for the second and third works.

If a collection contains four or more independent works that are entered under no more than three headings, apply the following:

1) If one heading is represented by one work, enter the collection under the uniform title for the first work or make an analytical added entry for it, as appropriate.

2) If one heading is represented by one excerpt from one work, apply 1) above.

3) If one heading is represented by two or more consecutively numbered excerpts from one work, enter the collection under the uniform title for the excerpts (25.6B1) or make an analytical added entry for them, as appropriate.

4) If one heading is represented by two unnumbered or nonconsecutively numbered excerpts from one work, enter the collection under the uniform title for the first excerpt (25.6B2) and make an analytical added entry for the other excerpt; or, make an analytical added entry for each excerpt, as appropriate.

 5) If one heading is represented by three or more unnumbered or nonconsecutively numbered excerpts from one work, enter the collection under the uniform title for the excerpts (25.6B3) or make an analytical added entry for them, as appropriate.

6) If one heading is represented by two works, enter the collection under the uniform title for the first work and make an analytical added entry for the other work; or make an analytical added entry for each work, as appropriate.

7) If one heading is represented by excerpts from two works, apply 2-5 above to each work.

8) If one personal name heading is represented by three or more works, enter the collection under an appropriate collective uniform title (e.g., "Selections") or make an analytical added entry under this uniform title as appropriate.

9) If one corporate name heading is represented by three or more works, enter the collection under the heading appropriate to the first work, but do not make any analytical added entries for the others; or, make an added entry for the name heading alone, as appropriate.

If a collection contains four or more independent works that are entered under four or more different headings, enter the collection under the heading for the work named first in the chief source. Generally do not make added entries for the other works.

Sound recordings

If a sound recording collection contains no more than fifteen music works entered under two or more different headings, enter the collection under the first work and make analytical added entries for the other works. Do not make analytical added entries for sound recording collections that are covered by the excluded categories in RI 21.7B [above]. (*CSB* 28:15-16)

COLLECTIVE UNIFORM TITLES AND ANALYTICAL ADDED ENTRIES

25.35-25.36 MCD Do not apply the following provisions to collections of pop, folk, ethnic, or jazz music or to multipart collections that are not yet complete. For excerpts from one work, treat each excerpt the same as a separate work unless there are two or more excerpts numbered consecutively (25.6B1) or three or more unnumbered or nonconsecutively numbered excerpts (25.6B3).

If a music publication or manuscript contains four or more works entered under a single personal name heading, and all the works but one form a group for which a collective uniform title naming a type (25.36B-C) would be appropriate, enter the collection under the collective uniform title appropriate to the item as a whole. Make a name-title analytical added entry for the group and one for the single work.

```
Chopin, Frederic
    [Piano music.  Selections]
    Scherzi ; und, Phantasie f Moll ...
```

Added entries: Chopin ... Scherzos, piano
                           Chopin ... Fantasie, piano, op. 49, F minor

If a music publication or manuscript contains six or more works entered under a single personal name heading, and the works may be divided into two groups of three or more works, for each of which a collective uniform title naming a type (25.36B-C) would be appropriate, enter the collection under the collective uniform title appropriate to the item as a whole. Make a name-title analytical added entry for each group.

```
Scriabin, Aleksandr Nikolaevich
    [Piano music.  Selections]
    The complete preludes & etudes : for pianoforte solo ...
```

Added entries: Scriabin ... Preludes, piano
                           Scriabin ... Etudes, piano

(*MCB* 13:1:6-7)

25.35-25.36 RI   If a sound recording collection contains three, four, or five musical works entered under a single personal name heading, enter the collection under the collective uniform title appropriate to the whole item. Make name-title analytical added entries for each work in the collection. For excerpts from one work, make a separate analytical added entry for each excerpt unless there are two or more excerpts numbered consecutively (25.6B1) or three or more unnumbered or nonconsecutively numbered excerpts (25.6B3). (*CSB* 13:48)

Do not apply these provisions to the following sound recording collections:
1) a collection whose contents consist of all of a composer's works of a particular type or of a particular type for a particular medium of performance (25.36B);

2) a collection made up of a consecutively numbered group of works (25:36C);

3) collections of pop, folk, ethnic, or jazz music;

4) multipart collections that are not yet complete.
(*MCB* 17:12:3)

25.35-25.36 MCD   If a sound recording collection contains six or more works entered under a single personal name heading, enter the collection under the collective uniform title appropriate to the item as a whole. Make name-title analytical added entries as follows:

1) If the works may be divided into no more than five groups of three or more works, for each of which a collective uniform title naming a type (25.36B-C) would be appropriate, make an analytical added entry for each group.

```
Chopin, Frederic
    [Piano music.  Selections]
    Waltzes ; and, Scherzos ...
```

Added entries:
```
          Chopin ... Waltzes, piano
          Chopin ... Scherzos, piano
```

2) If some of the works can be grouped as in (1) above and others cannot, and the groups and the remaining individual works together add up to five or less, make an analytical added entry for each group and for each of the remaining works.

```
Saint-Saëns, Camille
    [Orchestra music.  Selections]
    Symphonies ; & Tone poems [sound recording] ...
```

Added entries:
```
          Saint-Saëns ... Symphonies, no. 1-3
          Saint-Saëns ... Symphonic poems
          Saint-Saëns ... Marche heroique
```

3) If neither (1) nor (2) above can be applied but one of the works is featured, make an analytical added entry for that work; in addition make an analytical added entry under the collective uniform title appropriate to the remaining works if it is different from that used in the main entry.

```
Glinka, Mikhail Ivanovich
    [Instrumental music.  Selections]
    Trio pathétique : in D minor for clarinet, bassoon, and piano ;
    Selected piano works [sound recording] ...
```

Added entries:
```
          Glinka ... Trio pathétique
          Glinka ... Piano music.  Selections
```

```
Reger, Max
   [Chamber music.  Selections]
   Chamber music [sound recording] ...
```

(Contains the String quartet, op. 109 (55 min.), and various short works for clarinet and piano or violoncello and piano (10 min. total))

Added entry: `Reger ... Quartets, strings, op. 109, E``b major`

For references for collections without a collective title, see MCD 26.4C3 [below]. (*MCB* 13:1:7; 17:5:1-2)

COLLECTIONS OF WORKS ALL HAVING THE SAME TITLE

25.35-25.36 MCD See under *Collective Uniform Titles -- With the Same Title That is not the Name of a Type of Composition* above.

If the collection is a sound recording, make name-title analytical added entries according to RI 25.35-25.36 and the remainder of MCD 25.35-25.36 above. For references for collections without a collective title, see MCD 26.4C3 [below]. (*MCB* 13:1:7-8)

TITLE ADDED ENTRIES

21.30J MCD Follow the instructions in RI 21.30J (cf. *CSB* 18:37-46) in making title added entries for music publications and music sound recordings, disregarding the restriction in rule 21.30J(4). Exception: For items entered under the heading for a composer, do not make an added entry under a title that is not sufficiently distinctive by itself to be a useful access point (e.g., Piano music; Symphony no. 3 in F major, op. 90).

For collections without a collective title, trace separate title added entries for each of the titles listed in the title and statement of responsibility area, subject to the exception above. If the first title is to be traced, trace it explicitly using the "Title:" technique whenever it is not followed by a parallel title, other title information, or a statement of responsibility; otherwise, trace it using the "Title." technique (cf. RI 21.30J: 2. Items without a collective title [*CSB* 20:21-22]).

```
Transcription:  Die kleine Kammermusik ; Sonata in A minor ;
     L'hiver ; Naise ; Napolitana ; Air trompette ...
Title a.e.:  I. Title: Kleine Kammermusik.  II. Title:  Hiver.
     III. Title:  Naise.  IV. Title:  Napolitana.

Transcription:  Flos campi : for viola, voices, and orchestra (six
     movements segue) ; Suite for viola and orchestra ...
Title a.e.:  I. Title.

Transcription:  Piano concerto in A minor, op. 54 ;  Waldscenen :
     op. 82 ...
Title a.e.:  I. Title: Waldscenen.
```

When a title that is to be traced contains a number, follow the instruction in RI 21.30J: [9]. Numbers [*CSB* 20:25-27]. In addition, when such a title begins with a number that is not an integral part of the title, make an added entry under the title with the number omitted.

```
Title Proper:  5 romances sans paroles
Title a.e:  I. Title.  II. Title: Cinq romances sans paroles.
     III. Title:  Romances sans paroles.
```

(*MCB* 14:10:3; 17:7:2)

Note that initial articles have been deleted in the title added entries formulated according to the Music Cataloging Decision above. This is a result of constraints in the Library of Congress' machine-readable catalog.

RELATED PERSONS AND WORKS

21.30F MCD   Make an added entry for any person mentioned in the title proper or other title information of a bibliographic record for a musical work or collection. Exception: do not make an added entry if the person's relationship to the item is purely a subject relationship.

> Liszt, Franz
>   Präludium und Fuge über den Namen Bach ...
>
> *Added entry*: Bach, Johann Sebastian

(*MCB* 16:3:4)

21.30G MCD   When an instrumental work or collection is based on, inspired by, etc., one or two individual literary works, make a related-work added entry or entries (cf. RI 21.30M [*CSB* 20:12-14] for the literary work or works. (For vocal works based on literary works, see 21.19A.)

> Tchaikovsky, Peter Ilich
>   [Romeo et Juliette (Fantasy-overture)]
>   Romeo und Julia : Fantasie-Ouvertüre nach Shakespeare ...
>
> *Added entry*: Shakespeare, William. Romeo and Juliet.

When an instrumental work or collection is based on, inspired by, etc., three or more literary works by the same author, or an author's oeuvre in general, make an added entry for the author.

> Henze, Hans Werner
>   [Royal winter music. No. 1]
>   Royal winter music. First sonata on Shakespearean characters ...
>
> *Added entry*: Shakespeare, William

When a musical work is based on, inspired by, etc., one or more works by an artist, or an artist's oeuvre in general, make an added entry of the artist.

> Mussorgsky, Modest Petrovich
>   [Kartinki s vystavki]
>   Pictures at an exhibition ...
>   Note: Suite, based on paintings and drawings by Victor Hartmann.
>
> *Added entry*: Gartman, Viktor Aleksandrovich

(*MCB* 16:3:4-5)

REFERENCES

In general, follow the instructions in chapters 21 through 26 and exercise judgment in making references, particularly from forms of titles not used as uniform titles. Specific and detailed Library of Congress policy statements follow. (Note in the statements that follow, that LC displays "see" references with the term "search under.")

PERFORMING GROUPS

26.3B MCD   When the name of a performing group contains the name(s) of one or more persons connected with it, make see also reference(s) from the heading(s) for the person(s) to the heading for the group.

```
        Ashbury Stabbins Duo.
           xx   Ashbury, Roy
           xx   Stabbins, Larry

        Crosby, Stills & Nash
           xx   Crosby, David
           xx   Nash, Graham
           xx   Stills, Stephen

        Gary Burton Quartet
           xx   Burton, Gary
```

       (*MCB* 14:10:4)

DIFFERENT TITLES OR VARIANTS OF THE TITLE

        For the same reasons that make uniform titles so critically important in organizing access to musical works, the potential for multiple manifestations of a given work appearing under different titles proper makes references between the titles not chosen and the authorized uniform title equally critical. The following Library of Congress Music Cataloging Decisions provide detailed instructions for constructing references in such cases. Important principles to bear in mind are: 1) references should be made in the form in which they would appear had they been used as the uniform title; and, 2) because of the frequent use in music publications of titles that include names of types of composition, additions will sometimes be required to distinguish a reference under a composer heading from another work with a similar title that has been used as an authorized uniform title.
        In the instructions that follow, the phrase "cataloger-generated reference" refers to cases where a phrase other than the traditional "see" or "see also" (or, "search under" or "search also under") has been supplied by the cataloger who established the reference.

26.4A1 MCD   INTRODUCTION

        The following instructions deal with the choice and form of the title portion of name-title references for parts of works prescribed in rule 25.32A1. When references not in conformity with these instructions are encountered in a name authority record, they should be changed to conform if the record is being changed for another reason.

        Generally, the heading referred to should include only the basic uniform title of the work, without additions such as "arr." (25.31B2), "Vocal score" (25.31B3), "Libretto" (25.31B5), language (25.31B6-B7), etc., even if such additions are used in the uniform title in the bibliographic record of the item being cataloged. If, however, the title being referred from is specific to the arrangement, format, language, etc., brought out by an addition to the uniform title, and the title would not logically be used for a different manifestation of the work, refer to the uniform title with the addition.

```
        Bartok, Bela
           Kekszakallu herceg vara
           x  Bartok, Bela
                 Duke Bluebeard's castle
```

not:

```
Bartok, Bela
    Kekszakallu herceg vara.  English
    x  Bartok, Bela
           Duke Bluebeard's castle
```

but:

```
 John, Elton
     Crocodile rock.  Text
     x  John, Elton
            Words of Elton's smash hit "Crocodile Rock"
```

For further information regarding arrangements, see below under NON-DISTINCTIVE TITLES [section 4].

Underlying these instructions is the principle that each reference should, to the extent possible, be constructed, "in the same form in which it would be constructed if used as the heading" (RI 26.0 [*CSB* 32:47-50]). Thus, for example, it is understood that if a title being referred from begins with an article in the nominative case, the article should be omitted in accordance with RI 25.3A (2) [below].

The instructions are divided into two parts: the first for references from distinctive titles and the second for references from non-distinctive titles. Essentially, consider a title to be non-distinctive if it fits the description in the first paragraph of rule 5.1B1 as revised (cf. RI 5.1B1 (1) [above]). Consider other titles to be distinctive.

DISTINCTIVE TITLES

When the title proper of a work (or the principal title if a secondary entry is being made for the work in question) is distinctive and is significantly different from the work's uniform title, make a reference from it to the uniform title. Generally do not include other title information in the title referred from. Apply the criteria in rule 21.2A to determine whether a title is considered to be significantly different from the uniform title.

Similarly, refer from any other distinctive and significantly different title under which catalog users are likely to search for the work: e.g., a parallel title, especially one in English; an alternative title or a subtitle that has the nature of an alternative title; a nickname; the original title. Such titles may appear in the item being cataloged or may be found in a reference source; generally, however, do not do research solely for the purpose of identifying titles from which references should be made.

```
Sullivan, Arthur, Sir
    Patience
    x  Sullivan, Arthur, Sir
           Bunthorne's bride

Mendelssohn-Bartholdy, Felix
    Symphonies, no. 4, op. 90, A major
    x  Mendelssohn-Bartholdy, Felix
           Italian symphony
```

```
Schubert, Franz
    Moments musicaux
    x   Schubert, Franz
            Momens musicals
```
(Preface of the item being cataloged indicates the work was originally published under the title "Momens musicals")

CONFLICTS

When a distinctive title to be referred from is the same as the uniform title of another work entered under the same composer (apart from any additions made to that uniform title under rule 25.31B1), resolve the conflict by making an addition or additions to the reference according to 25.31B1. Change the existing uniform title by making a corresponding addition or additions to it, if it does not already include them.

```
Bach, Johann Sebastian
    Gott, der Herr, is Sonn' und Schild.  Nun danket alle Gott
    x   Bach, Johann Sebastian
            Nun danket alle Gott (Chorale), BMV 79, no. 3
```
(Established uniform title: [Nun danket alle gott (Cantata)])
(The index to Schmeider lists six works or parts of works with the title "Nun danket alle Gott": one cantata, three chorales, one chorale prelude, and one motet)

```
Schubert, Franz
    Quartets, strings, D. 810, D minor
    x   Schubert, Franz
            Tod und das Mädchen (String quartet)
```
(Established uniform title: [Tod und das Mädchen], to be changed to [Tod und das Madchen (Song)])

When a distinctive title to be referred from is the same as the title in a name-title reference to another work by the same composer, resolve the conflict by making additions to both references according to rule 25.31B1.

```
Beethoven, Ludwig van
    Ouvertüre zur Oper Leonore, no. 1
    x   Beethoven, Ludwig van
            Leonore overture, no. 1

Beethoven, Ludwig van
    Fidelio (1806).  Overture
    x   Beethoven, Ludwig van
            Leonore overture, no. 3

Gliere, Reinhold Moritsevich
    P´esy, op. 35.  Grustnyi val´s
    x   Gliere, Reinhold Moritsevich
            Valse triste, clarinet, piano

Gliere, Reinhold Moritsevich
    P´esy, pianos (2), op. 41.  Grustnyi val´s
    x   Gliere, Reinhold Moritsevich
            Valse triste, pianos (2)
```

If, however, the works can be clearly identified from the references (taking both the refer-from and the refer-to portions into consideration) without making additions to the title being referred from, do not make the additions.

```
Debussy, Claude
     Images, orchestra
   x  Debussy, Claude
          Obrazy

Debussy, Claude
     Images, piano
   x  Debussy, Claude
          Obrazy
```

VARIANT FORMS OF TITLES

1. *Ampersand.* When an ampersand (or other symbol, e.g. +, representing the word "and") occurs as one of the first five words filed on in a distinctive uniform title or in a distinctive title being referred from, make a reference (or an additional reference) substituting the word "and" in the language of the title.

```
Green, David Llewellyn
     Allegro moderato & three metamorphoses
   x   Green, David Llewellyn
           Allegro moderato and three metamorphoses
   x   Green, David Llewellyn
           Allegro moderato & drei Metamorphosen
   x   Green, David Llewellyn
           Allegro moderato und drei Metamorphosen
```

2. *Numbers.* When a number occurs as one of the first five words filed on in a distinctive uniform title or in a distinctive title being referred from, make references (or additional references) according to the principles governing the making of added entries set forth in RI 21.30J (7-10) [*CSB* 27:24-28]. In addition, when a distinctive title being referred from begins with a number that is not an integral part of the title, make a reference from the title with the number omitted (unless the resulting title is the same as the uniform title).

```
Bach, Johann Sebastian
     Brandenburgische Konzerte
   x   Bach, Johann Sebastian
           6 concerti brandesburghesi
   x   Bach, Johann Sebastian
           Sei concerti brandesburghesi
   x   Bach, Johann Sebastian
           Concerti brandesburghesi
```

3. *Other.* If a distinctive title proper or a distinctive title being referred from contains data within the first five words filed on for which there could be an alternative form that would be filed differently, make a reference (or an additional reference) from that form if it is thought that some users of the catalog might reasonably search under that form, following the guidelines for title added entries in RI 21.30J(3-11) [*CSB* 27:23-28].

NON-DISTINCTIVE TITLES

Make references based on non-distinctive titles only when the uniform title that would result from the application of 25.26-25.31A (and 25.31B2 when appropriate) to such a title is different from the actual uniform title. Then make a reference only in the form that the uniform title would take if the title in question had been selected as the basis of the uniform title. The following examples illustrate the most typical situations in which references based on non-distinctive titles are needed.

1. The title selected as the basis for the uniform title is distinctive but the work is also known by a non-distinctive title.

```
Hovhaness, Alan
    Artik
    x  Hovhaness, Alan
            Concertos, horn, string orchestra, op. 78
```

2. The work is also known by the name of a type of composition different from that selected as the basis for the uniform title.

```
Pleyel, Ignaz
    Sonatas, piano trio, B. 465-467
    x  Pleyel, Ignaz
            Trios, piano, strings, B. 465-467
```

3. The work is identified in the item being cataloged by a number from a numbering system different from that used in the uniform title.

```
Dvorak, Antonin
    Symphonies, no. 8, op. 88, G major
    x  Dvorak, Antonin
            Symphonies, no. 4, op. 88, G major

Haydn, Joseph
    Symphonies, H. I, 6, D major
    x  Haydn, Joseph
            Symphonies, no. 6, D major

Vivaldi, Antonio
    Concertos, oboes (2), continuo, RV 535, D minor
    x  Vivaldi, Antonio
            Concertos, oboes (2), continuo, op. 42, no. 2, D
    minor
    x  Vivaldi, Antonio
            Concertos, oboes (2), continuo, P. 302, D minor
```
(Title on item being cataloged: Concerto for two oboes and bassoon in D minor, op. 42, no. 2, P. 302)

(Generally do not refer from titles using numbers not found in the item being cataloged unless such numbers originated with the composer.)

4. The item being cataloged is published for a medium of performance other than the original, and a statement of medium of performance would be required in the uniform title if the version being cataloged were the original version.

```
Boccherini, Luigi
    Quintets, flute, violins, viola, violoncello, G. 436, D minor
    x  Boccherini, Luigi
            Quintets, oboe, violins, viola, violoncello, G. 436,
    D minor
```

```
Pleyel, Ignaz
    Quartets, flute, violin, viola, violoncello, B. 386, C major;
arr.
    x  Pleyel, Ignaz
          Trios, clarinets, bassoon, op. 20. No. 1
```

CONFLICTS

When a title in a reference formulated in uniform-title format according to these instructions is the same as the uniform title of another work entered under the same composer, resolve the conflict by making an addition or additions to the reference according to rule 25.31A6. Also change the existing uniform title by making a corresponding addition or additions.

```
Hindemith, Paul
    Sonatas, alto horn, piano
    x  Hindemith, Paul
          Sonatas, horn, piano (1943)
(For alto horn, horn, or saxophone and piano)
(Established uniform title:  [Sonatas, horn, piano], to be changed to [Sonatas,
    horn, piano (1939)]
```

If the application of these instructions results in two identical references to different uniform titles entered under the same composer, resolve the conflict by making an addition or additions to each reference according to rule 25.31A6. (*MCB* 15:10:3-6; 17:5:2)

PARTS OF A WORK

26.4A3 MCD When appropriate, name-title references may be made to the uniform title for a part of a work from the uniform title of the work followed by a variant title of the part.

```
    Rossini, Gioacchino
        Semiramide.  Overture
    search under
    Rossini, Gioacchino
        Semiramide.  Sinfonia
```

(unpublished RI)

COLLECTIVE UNIFORM TITLES

26.4A4 MCD When the title proper (or other title being referred from) of a collection of, or selection from, a composer's works is identical with a uniform title that has been used under the heading for that composer in a bibliographic record or name authority record in the catalog, trace the name-title reference from the bibliographic title to the collective uniform title as a "see-also" reference.

```
    Schubert, Franz
        An die Musik
    search also under.
    Schubert, Franz
        Songs.  Selections
(Established uniform title:  [An die Musik])
```

```
        Boyce, William
            Concerti grossi
        search also under
     Boyce, William
            Instrumental music.  Selections
     (Established uniform title:   [Concerti grossi])
```

In all other cases, trace the reference as a "see" reference.

```
        Ellington, Duke
            Sophisticated lady
        search under
     Ellington, Duke
            Songs.  Selections
     (Uniform title [Sophisticated lady] not established)
```

```
        Baksa, Robert F.
            Chamber music
        search under
     Baksa, Robert F.
            Instrumental music.  Selections
     (Uniform title [Chamber music] not established)
```

When a uniform title is established (i.e. used in an NAR [name-authority record] or a bibliographic record) which is identical with a title in a name-title "see" reference under the same composer, change the reference to a "see also" reference.

For references to collective uniform titles for sound recordings without a collective title containing three or more works by a single composer, see MCD 26.4C3 [below]. (*MCB* 17:5:2)

26.4C3 MCD For a collection without a collective title containing three or more works entered under a single personal name heading, make a cataloger-generated name-title reference from the transcribed title of the first work to the collective uniform title of the collection, using the legend "For a collection beginning with this title search under" (or "... search also under "), if no analytical added entry is made for the first work. (If an analytical added entry is made for the first work, sufficient access to the bibliographic record is provided by that analytical added entry and associated references.)

If the title being referred from is identical with a uniform title that has been used under the heading for the composer in a bibliographic record or name authority record in the catalog, treat the reference as a "see also" cataloger-generated reference; otherwise treat it as a "see" cataloger-generated reference.

```
        Chopin, Frederic
            Allegro de concert
        For a collection beginning with this title search also
            under
     Chopin, Frederic
            Instrumental music.  Selections
     (Established uniform title:   [Allegro de concert])
```

```
        Debussy, Claude
            Cathédrale engloutie
        For a collection beginning with this title search under
     Debussy, Claude
            Piano music.  Selections
     (Established uniform title:   [Preludes, piano, book 1  Cathédrale
         engloutie])
```

When a uniform title is established (i.e., used in an NAR or a bibliographic record) which is identical with a title in a name-title "see" reference under the same composer, change the reference to a "see also" reference.

When a cataloger-generated reference to a collective uniform title is encountered that is known not to be in conformity with these instructions, cancel it if the NAR is being changed for another reason. (*MCB* 15:9:2; 17:5:2)

DISTINCTIVE TITLES IN DIFFERENT LANGUAGES -- VARIANT MANIFESTATIONS

In general, refer from different language forms of a distinctive uniform title only to the uniform title for the work as a whole. For instance, when cataloging a vocal score of Wagner's *Flying Dutchman* (uniform title: `Fliegende Hollander. Vocal score. English`) refer from the English form to the original title of the whole work.

```
Wagner, Richard
    Flying Dutchman
see
Wagner, Richard
    Fliegende Hollander
```

An exception is made when the work in hand is an arrangement.

```
Pleyel, Ignaz
    Serenade no. 1 in D major for two oboes, two clarinets,
two horns, and two bassoons
see
Pleyel, Ignaz
    Quartets, strings, B. 321. F major;  arr.
```

When necessary to make the reference clear or distinctive, include also the other title information in the reference.

```
Mozart, Wolfgang Amadeus
    Highlights of The marriage of Figaro, arranged for E-Z
organ
see
Mozart, Wolfgang Amadeus
    Nozze di Figaro. Selections;  arr.
```

(*Bibliographic description*: `Highlights of The marriage of Figaro  : arranged for E-Z organ ... )`

```
Schubert, Franz
    Romanze, for soprano, clarinet, and piano
see
Schubert, Franz
    Verschworenen. Romanze;  arr.
```

(*Bibliographic description*: `Romanze for soprano, clarinet, and piano ... )`

(cf. *MCB* 13:11:3-4)

CHAPTER 5: CATALOGING EXAMPLES

MOZART

SYMPHONY № 40
G MINOR (K 550)

M. BARON, INC. NEW YORK

I.	Allegro molto	6 min.	Page 3
II.	Andante	9 min.	Page 21
III.	Allegretto	4 min.	Page 32
IV.	Allegro assai	7 min.	Page 35

№ 17
PRINTED IN U.S.A.

(On verso back cover:
Baron Orchestra Scores)

NOTE:
*For original version omit lines 1 and 2.
For Mozart's subsequent version omit line 4 (oboes).

MB 17

Printed in USA

(51 p. ; 21 cm.)

("MB 17" appears at the foot of each page)

```
Mozart, Wolfgang Amadeus, 1756-1791.
   [Symphonies, K. 550, G minor]
   Symphony no. 40, G minor, K 550 / Mozart. -- New York : M.
Baron, [19--]
   1 miniature score (51 p.) ; 21 cm. -- (Baron orchestra scores ; no.
no. 17)

   Duration: 26:00.
   Pl. no.: MB 17.
```

Symphony is the name of a type of composition, so the statements of serial and thematic index enumeration and the key are included in the title proper. The musical notation is printed in a reduced format, making performance use unlikely, so this item is described as "miniature score" in the physical description area. The number "MB 17", which appears at the foot of each page (i.e. on each plate) of music, is a plate number.

Main entry is under the heading for Mozart, the composer. There are no added entries. (The title is not traced because it fits the provisions of 21.29J(4); the series is not traced because it fits the provision of 21.30L(1).)

The uniform title is based on Mozart's original *Eine Sinfonie* (Cf. Koechel *Verzeichnis*). Because it is the name of a type of composition ("Symphony") that is cognate in English, French, German, and Italian, and because Mozart wrote more than one work of this type, the term is used in its English plural form in the uniform title. The medium of performance is not added because it is implicit (full orchestra) in the name of the type of composition. The serial enumeration is dropped in deference to the thematic index number (K. 550). The key is added as the last element.

Copyright, 1895, by G. Schirmer, Inc.   Copyright
12117   Printed in the

(On cover: *G. Schirmer's Vocal Scores of Grand and Light Operas*. Also on cover: "With French and English texts." Portrait of Bizet faces title page. 391 p. ; 28 cm.)

("12117" appears at the foot of each page of the score)

CARMEN

Opera in Four Acts

By

GEORGES BIZET

Words by

H. MEILHAC and L. HALEVY

Adapted from the Novel by
PROSPER MÉRIMÉE

English Version by
DR. TH. BAKER

G. SCHIRMER, Inc., NEW YORK

```
Bizet, Georges, 1838-1875.
    [Carmen.  Vocal score.  English & French]
    Carmen : opera in four acts / by Georges Bizet ; words by H.
Meilhac and L. Halévy ; adapted from the novel by Prosper Mérimée ;
English version by Th. Baker. -- New York : G. Schirmer, c1895.
    1 vocal score (391 p.) : port. ; 28 cm. -- (G. Schirmer's vocal
scores of grand and light operas)

    French and English words.
    Pl. no.: 12117.


    I. Meilhac, Henri, 1831-1897.  II. Halévy, Ludovic, 1834-1908.
III. Baker, Theodore, 1851-1934.  IV. Mérimée, Prosper, 1803-1870.
Carmen.  V. Title.
```

The title *Carmen* is not the name of a type of composition, so all extraneous title page data are considered to be other title information. The copyright date is not bracketed because it appears at the foot of the first page of music. The original orchestral accompaniment has been arranged for the piano, so this item is described as "1 vocal score."

Main entry is under the heading for Bizet, the composer. Added entries are required for Meilhac and Halévy as authors of the libretto and for Baker as author of the English version (which is not a strict translation). An author-title added entry is made under the heading for Mérimée's novel. The series is once again disregarded because of 21.30L(1).

The uniform title is the composer's original title, unaltered because it is "distinctive." Additions are made to indicate the physical manifestation "Vocal score" and the languages of the translated and original texts (both present in the item), "English & French."

Deux Cadences
pour le 4ᵉ Concerto, Op. 58
de BEETHOVEN

I

I. MOSCHELÈS

(The cover and list title page
are printed from the same
printing surface. 7 p. ; 32 cm.)

ÉDITION CLASSIQUE A. DURAND & FILS

I. MOSCHELÈS

CADENCES
pour les concertos de piano
de BEETHOVEN

Doigtées et révisées

PAR

I. PHILIPP
Professeur au Conservatoire National de Paris

Nº 10473 — DEUX CADENCES POUR LE CONCERTO EN UT MAJEUR (op. 15)   net : 1.50

Nº 10474 — CADENCE POUR LE CONCERTO EN SI BÉMOL (op. 19) . . . . .   — 1.50

Nº 10475 — CADENCE POUR LE CONCERTO EN UT MINEUR (op. 37) . . . .   — 1.50

Nº 10476 — DEUX CADENCES POUR LE CONCERTO EN SOL (op. 58) . . . .   — 1.50

Paris, A. DURAND & FILS, Éditeurs.
DURAND & Cⁱᵉ
4, Place de la Madeleine

Déposé selon les traités internationaux. Propriété pour tous pays.
Tous droits d'exécution, de traduction, de reproduction et d'arrangements réservés

D. & F. 10,476

Paris, 4, Place de la Madeleine

```
Moschelès, Ignaz, 1794-1870.
   Deux cadences pour le 4e concerto, op. 58 de Beethoven / I.
Moschelès. -- Paris : Durand, c1924.
   7 p. of music ; 32 cm. -- (Cadences pour les concertos de piano de
Beethoven / I. Moschelès) (Editions classique A. Durand & fils)

   Caption title.
   Revised and fingered by I. Philipp.
   Pl. no.: D. & F. 10, 476.

   I. Philipp, Isidore, 1863-1958. II. Beethoven, Ludwig van, 1770-
1827.  Concertos, piano, orchestra, no. 4, op. 58, G major. III.
Series: Moschelès, Ignaz, 1794-1870.  Cadenzen zu Beethoven'schen
Klavierkonzerten (1924).
```

Cadences, or Cadenzas, is the name of a type of composition, so all the extraneous detail is included in the title proper. The caption is used as the chief source of information because it provides slightly more information than the list title page. Because this music is for solo piano it cannot be described as "score," and so it is described as "p. of music" in the physical description area. Isidore Philipp's name is not interpolated into the statement of responsibility area because it appears on the title page in a position related to the series, rather than in a position relative to the item being cataloged. As a result, his name is given in a note.

Main entry is under the heading for Moschelès, the composer of the cadenzas (cadenzas rarely require uniform titles). Added entries are required for Philipp, whose editorial contribution was substantial, and for the Beethoven concerto for which these two cadenzas were composed.

The Moschelès series was originally published in four volumes by B. Senff, Leipzig, with the title *Cadenzen zu Beethoven'schen Klavierkonzerten;* consequently a uniform title must be formulated for the series entered under the name heading for Moschelès. Although this title includes the name of a type of composition, it does not consist *solely* of the name of that type, so the original title is treated as a distinctive title and used unchanged. The date of publication of the Durand edition is added in parentheses to distinguish this version from the original (see RI 25.5B). The other series is disregarded because of 25.30L(1).

Boris Blacher

Op. 58

Requiem

Klavierauszug mit Text

Gegr. 1838

BOTE & BOCK

BERLIN · WIESBADEN

Imprimé en Allemagne   Printed in Germany

(On verso title page: Copyright 1959 ... On Contents
page: Spieldauer: ca. 45 Minuten. In caption on first
page of music : für Sopran- und Bariton-Solo, gemischten
Chor und Orchester. 104 p. ; 31 cm.)

Aufführungsrecht vorbehalten
© Copyright 1959 by Bote & Bock, Berlin

Eigentum der Verleger für alle Länder

B & B
21529
(741)

Bote & Bock, Berlin

92

```
Blacher, Boris, 1903-1975.
   [Requiem, op. 58.  Vocal score.  Latin]
   Requiem op. 58 / Boris Blacher ; Klavierauszug mit Text. -- Berlin
: Bote & Bock, c1959.
   1 vocal score (104 p.) ; 31 cm.

   For solo voices (SBar), chorus (SSAATTBB), and orchestra; acc. arr
for piano.
   Duration: ca. 45:00.
   Pl. no.: B & B 21529.
```

Requiem is the name of a type of composition, so the opus number is included as part of the title proper. The musical presentation statement "Klavierauszug mit Text" (i.e., "piano version with words") implies responsibility because it indicates that the accompaniment has been arranged for piano. Therefore, it is transcribed in the statement of responsibility area, even though no name is associated with it. The orchestral accompaniment has been arranged for piano, so this item is described as "1 vocal score" in the physical description area. This fact its highlighted again in the note on the medium of performance.

Main entry is under the heading for Blacher, the composer. No added entries are required.

The uniform title is based on Blacher's original, which is used unaltered because it is: 1) the name of a type of composition; and, 2) cognate in English, French, German and Italian. It is not given in a plural form because Blacher wrote only one work of this type. The medium of performance (chorus, soloists, and orchestra) is implicit in the name of the type of composition, so it is not added to the uniform title. The opus number is added because it is the only available distinguishing element. The manifestation is indicated in the uniform title ("Vocal score") as well as the language "Latin" because the title *Requiem* is derived from a liturgical text.

(Includes 1 score for violin and continuo; one part for violin and one part for basso continuo. The score is 7 pages long. All three are 30 cm. in height.)

```
Handel, George Frideric, 1685-1759.
   [Sonatas, op. 1.   No. 3]
   Sonate A-dur, für Violine und Basso continuo / Georg Friedrich
Händel ; Gitarre-Continuo, Erwin Schaller. -- Wien : Doblinger,
c1971.
   1 score (7 p.) + 2 parts ; 30 cm. -- (Gitarre-Kammermusik ; Nr.
95)

   Unfigured bass realized for guitar; includes part for bass
instrument.
   Edited by Karl Scheit.
   Pl. no.: D. 14.000.

   I. Schaller, Erwin.  II. Scheit, Karl.  III. Series.
```

Once again, the statements of medium of performance and key are transcribed as part of the title proper because *Sonate* is the name of a type of composition. The musical presentation statement, "Gitarre-Continuo," is transcribed in the statement of responsibility area because it contains a personal name. In the physical description area, no pagination is given for the parts because they are not the same length; the pagination for the score is given. The editor's name is given in a note because it appears prominently on the first page of music.

Main entry is under the heading for Handel as composer. Added entries are made for Scheit, the editor, and Schaller, who altered the continuo part for guitar; these entries are dependent on the cataloger's judgment and may not be necessary in some catalogs. Schaller's contribution, in particular, is minimal; the continuo part is virtually the same as Handel's original. The series is traced.

The uniform title is complex. Handel wrote many sonatas for treble instruments and continuo, and this publication fails to specifically identify the sonata. A search through Bell's thematic catalog, comparing musical incipits, shows us that this is actually the third of a set of fifteen sonatas originally published as opus 1. Because that makes this work an excerpt, we must first establish the uniform title for opus 1, then establish the uniform title for this excerpt. Note in the thematic catalog that the first editions (and most modern editions, as well) were titled *Sonates*, though Handel's original title was *Solos*. *Sonatas* is used because it is a later, better known title in the same language as the composer's original. Because "sonata" is a type of composition, and is cognate in English, French, German, and Italian, and because Handel wrote more than one work of this type, the uniform title is based on the English plural form "Sonatas." No medium of performance is given because the medium is diverse, that is, the fifteen sonatas in opus 1 are not all for the same performing medium. The opus number is included as a distinguishing element. Thus the uniform title for the whole work is "Sonatas, op. 1."

The excerpt is identified in the uniform title by the addition of its number "No. 3," because all of the parts of opus 1 are identified by the title *Sonata*. "Arr." is not used because the music has not been altered.

SECHS DUETTE

aus Opern Georg Friedrich Händels

Ausgabe für zwei Singstimmen und Klavier

VEB Deutscher Verlag für Musik Leipzig

(44 p. ; 27 cm. The caption for each selection is made up of the quoted portions of the contents list. The number DVfm 9071 appears only on the first page of the score)

2. Auflage
VEB Deutscher Verlag für Musik Leipzig · 1976
Lizenznummer 418-515/C 826/76
Umschlagentwurf: Joachim Thamm, Leipzig
Printed in the German Democratic Republic
Druck und Bindearbeit: III/18/299
Bestellnummer DVfM 9071

DVfM 9071

Handel, George Frideric, 1685-1759.
　　[Operas.　Vocal scores.　Italian & German.　Selections]
　　Sechs Duette : aus Opern Georg Friedrich Händels / Ausgabe für zwei
Singstimmen und Klavier. -- 2. Aufl. -- Leipzig : Deutscher Verlag
für Musik, 1976, c1974.
　　1 vocal score (44 p.) ; 27 cm.

　　For solo voices (ST or SB) and piano.
　　Contents: Bramo haver mill vite : aus "Ariodante" -- Troppo
oltraggi la mia fede : aus "Xerxes" -- Dite spera : aus "Ariodante" -
-- Se mai turbo il tuo riposo : aus "Poros" -- Caro! Bella! : aus
"Julius Caesar."
　　Publisher's no.: DVfM 9071.

Though the title *Duette* is the name of a type of composition, the subordinate clause "aus Opern Georg Friedrich Handels" ("from the operas of Georg Friedrich Handel") is transcribed as other title information because it does not include a statement of medium of performance, key, or enumeration. It is not included in the statement of responsibility because it is grammatically part of the title. However, the musical presentation statement is included as a statement of responsibility because it implies alteration of the music. Note the different use made of the German words for "edition," "Ausgabe" and "Auflage." Because the original duets were for voices and orchestra, and the accompaniment in this item is for piano, the physical description uses the specific material designation "1 vocal score." The number "DVfM 9071" is transcribed as a publisher's number because it appears only in the preliminaries.

The main entry is under Handel as composer. There are no added entries.

Because this item contains excerpts from several works, the uniform title is based on the uniform title for the original works themselves. In this case all of the works are operas, so the first element of the uniform title is "Operas" (cf. 25.36B). The term "Vocal score" is added to indicate the physical manifestation. Because the words are presented in both the original Italian as well as in German translation, the languages are indicated in the uniform title. Finally "Selections" is added to show that the item contains three or more diverse excerpts.

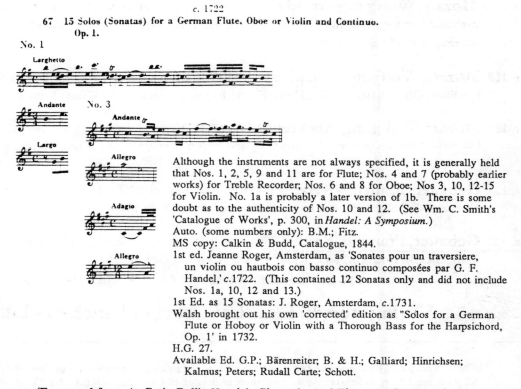

Although the instruments are not always specified, it is generally held that Nos. 1, 2, 5, 9 and 11 are for Flute; Nos. 4 and 7 (probably earlier works) for Treble Recorder; Nos. 6 and 8 for Oboe; Nos 3, 10, 12-15 for Violin. No. 1a is probably a later version of 1b. There is some doubt as to the authenticity of Nos. 10 and 12. (See Wm. C. Smith's 'Catalogue of Works', p. 300, in *Handel: A Symposium*.)
Auto. (some numbers only): B.M.; Fitz.
MS copy: Calkin & Budd, Catalogue, 1844.
1st ed. Jeanne Roger, Amsterdam, as 'Sonates pour un traversiere,
　　un violin ou hautbois con basso continuo composées par G. F.
　　Handel,' c.1722. (This contained 12 Sonatas only and did not include
　　Nos. 1a, 10, 12 and 13.)
1st Ed. as 15 Sonatas: J. Roger, Amsterdam, c.1731.
Walsh brought out his own 'corrected' edition as "Solos for a German
　　Flute or Hoboy or Violin with a Thorough Bass for the Harpsichord,
　　Op. 1' in 1732.
H.G. 27.
Available Ed. G.P.; Bärenreiter; B. & H.; Galliard; Hinrichsen;
　　Kalmus; Peters; Rudall Carte; Schott.

(Excerpted from A. Craig Bell's *Handel: Chronological Thematic Catalogue*)

LEUCKARTIANA

Alte Mufik

KLASSISCHE BLÄSERMUSIK

In Erstausgaben und praktischen Einrichtungen

Leuckartiana   Fortsetzung

Nr. 115 Danzi, Franz (1763-1826) **Bläserquintett F-Dur, op. 56,3** Für Flöte, Oboe, Klarinette (B),
Horn (F) und Fagott (Original) nach dem Erstdruck herausgegeben von Fritz Kneusslin

Nr. 116 Danzi, Franz (1763-1826) **Bläserquintett G-Dur, op. 67,1** Für Flöte, Oboe, Klarinette (A),
Horn (D) und Fagott (Original) nach dem Erstdruck herausgegeben von Werner Rottler

Nr. 117 Mozart, Wolfgang Amadeus (1756-1791) **Quintett c-moll (K.V. 406)**
nach dem Streichquintett (K.V. 406) für Flöte, Oboe, Klarinette (B), Horn (F) und Fagott
übertragen von Werner Rottler

Nr. 118 Mozart, Wolfgang Amadeus (1756-1791) **Divertimento Nr. 12 Es-Dur (K.V. 252)**
Für Flöte, Oboe, Klarinette (B), Horn (F) und Fagott übertragen von Werner Rottler

Nr. 119 Mozart, Wolfgang Amadeus (1756-1791) **Divertimento Nr. 16 Es-Dur (K.V. 289)**
Für Flöte, Oboe, Klarinette (B), Horn (F) und Fagott übertragen von Werner Rottler

Nr. 120 Gebauer, François-René (1773-1845) **Bläserquintett Nr. 2 Es-Dur** Für Flöte, Oboe,
Klarinette (B), Horn (Es) und Fagott herausgegeben von Udo Sirker

Nr. 121 Gebauer, François-René (1773-1845) **Bläserquintett Nr. 3 c-moll** Für Flöte, Oboe,
Klarinette (B), Horn (Es) und Fagott herausgegeben von Udo Sirker

EIGENTUM DES VERLEGERS FÜR ALLE LÄNDER

Verlag von F. E. C. Leuckart · München - Leipzig

(There is no score; there are five parts, one for each of the instruments named on the list title page.
All parts are 31 cm. in height. At the bottom of each page of each part: F.E.C.L. 10553. At the
bottom of the first page of each part: Copyright 1970 F. E. C. Leukart.)

Gebauer, Francois René, 1733-1845.
   [Quintets, winds, no. 3, C minor]
    Bläserquintett Nr. 3, c-moll, für Flöte, Oboe, Klarinette (B), Horn
(Es), und Fagott / Gebauer, Francois-René ; herausgegeben von Udo
Sirker. -- München : F.E.C. Leuckart, c1970.
    5 parts ; 31 cm. -- (Alte Musik. Klassische Bläsermusik ; Nr. 121)
(Leuckartiana)

    Cover title.
    Pl. no.: F.E.C.L. 10553.

    I. Sirker, Udo. II. Series: Alte Musik. Klassische Bläsermusik ;
Nr. 121.

   The cover of this set of parts presents a "list title page" that contains more complete information than any
of the captions of the parts. The entire title is transcribed as title proper because *Bläserquintett* (Wind quartet") is the
name of a type of composition. The composer's and editor's names are transposed into the statement of
responsibility because they are not grammatically linked to the title proper.

   Main entry is under Gebauer, the composer, with added entries for Sirker, the editor, as well as the series
Klassische Bläsermusik. Leuckartiana is not traced because of 21.30L(1).

   The uniform title is based on *Quintett*, which is the name of a type of composition, cognate in English,
French, German, and Italian, and here given in plural because Gebauer wrote more than one. "Winds" is used as the
statement of medium of performance, because the combination of flute, oboe, clarinet, horn and bassoon is one of
the standard chamber combinations listed in 25.29C (wind quintet). The serial number and key are added as
distinguishing element.

FIDELIO

OR

WEDDED LOVE

———

AN OPERA IN TWO ACTS

———

Words adapted from the French of
J. N. BOUILLY
by
J. F. SONNLEITHNER
and
F. TREITSCHKE

Music by
LUDWIG VAN BEETHOVEN

English version by
EDWARD J. DENT

OXFORD UNIVERSITY PRESS
London   New York   Toronto
1938

(xvi, 37 p., 19 cm.)

OPERA LIBRETTI
English Versions by EDWARD J. DENT

———

THE MAGIC FLUTE
THE MARRIAGE OF FIGARO
DON GIOVANNI
FIDELIO

Price 2s. net each
Other operas in preparation

(Kinsky lists this work as "Opus 72 Fidelio (Leonore)." The first edition of the score of the first verison ("Erste Fassung (1805)") was titled *Leonore*. The work was revised twice ("Zweite Fassung (1806)," "Dritte Fassung (1814)"). The 1814 version is the one that is usually performed today. Original editions, as well as the autograph, were titled *Fidelio*. Riemann lists the work as "Fidelio (Leonore)." This libretto contains the text for the 1814 version, translated into English. There is no music.)

```
Beethoven, Ludwig van, 1770-1827.
   [Fidelio (1814).  Libretto.  English]
   Fidelio, or, Wedded love : an opera in two acts /
words adapted from the French of J.N. Bouilly by
J.F.Sonnleithner and F. Treitschke ; music by Ludwig van
Beethoven ; English version by Edward J. Dent. -- London ;
New York : Oxford University Press, 1938.
   xvi, 37 p. ; 19 cm. -- (Opera libretti / English
versions by Edward J. Dent)
   Translation of: Fidelio, oder, Die eheliche Liebe,
adapted by Sonnleithner and rev. by Treitschke from
Bouilly's Léonore, ou, L'amour conjugal.

   I. Sonnleithner, Joseph Ferdinand, 1766-1835.  II.
Treitschke, Georg Friedrich, 1776-1842.  III. Dent, Edward
J. (Edward Joseph), 1876-1957.  IV. Bouilly, J. N. (Jean
Nicolas), 1763-1842.  Léonore.  V. Title.  VI. Title:
Fidelio.
```

Because this item is a libretto and contains no music per se, it is cataloged very much like a book. There is nothing particularly remarkable about the description.

Main entry is under the heading for the related work, Beethoven's opera *Fidelio*, according to the alternative rule at 21.28. Added entries are required for Sonnleithner and Treitschke who wrote the original libretto, Dent who wrote the English version presented in this item, and the Bouilly work from which the libretto was originally adapted. A separate title added entry is provided for *Fidelio* alone because the first title tracing will include the alternative title as well.

The uniform title is based on the title *Fidelio* because it was Beethoven's original title, and because it is the title by which the work is best known today. The qualifying date "(1814)" is added to indicate the particular version because Beethoven's revisions were extensive (cf. MCD 25.26B). A reference would be traced from "Beethoven ... Leonore (1814)" to "Beethoven ... Fidelio (1814)." The manifestation "Libretto" and the language of translation "English" are also indicated in the uniform title.

Lizenz-Nr. 472-155'332/57
Gesamtherstellung:
VEB Messe- und Musikaliendruck, Leipzig III/18/157

(Colophon)

(List title page)

JOH. SEB. BACH
KIRCHENKANTATEN
KLAVIERAUSZÜGE

Nr.		Nr.	
51.	Jauchzet Gott in allen Landen	75.	Die Elenden sollen essen
52.	Falsche Welt, dir trau ich nicht	76.	Die Himmel erzählen die Ehre Gottes
53.	Schlage doch, gewünschte Stunde	77.	Du sollst Gott, deinen Herrn lieben
54.	Widerstehe doch der Sünde	78.	Jesu, der du meine Seele
55.	Ich armer Mensch, ich Sündenknecht	79.	Gott der Herr ist Sonn und Schild
56.	Ich will den Kreuzstab gerne tragen	80.	Ein feste Burg ist unser Gott
57.	Selig ist der Mann	81.	Jesus schläft, was soll ich hoffen?
58.	Ach Gott, wie manches Herzeleid	82.	Ich habe genug
	(2. Komposition)	83.	Erfreute Zeit im neuen Bunde
59.	Wer mich liebet, der wird mein Wort	84.	Ich bin vergnügt in meinem Glücke
	halten (1. Komposition)	85.	Ich bin ein guter Hirt
60.	O Ewigkeit, du Donnerwort	86.	Wahrlich, ich sage euch
	(2. Komposition)	87.	Bisher habt ihr nichts gebeten in
61.	Nun komm, der Heiden Heiland		meinem Namen
	(1. Komposition)	88.	Siehe, ich will viel Fischer aussenden,

Nr. 78

Jesu, der du meine Seele

Jesus, my beloved Saviour

(BWV 78)

Breitkopf & Härtel,
Leipzig.

...XVERLAG

Printed in Germany

(Cover)

Bach, Johann Sebastian, 1685-1750.
    [Jesu, der du meine Seele (Cantata). Vocal score. English &
German]
    Kantate Nr. 78 : am vierzehnten Sonntage nach Trinitatis,
Jesu, der du meine Seele : für Sopran-, Alt-, Tenor-, Bass-
Solo und Chor (BWV 78) = Cantata no. 78 : for the fourteenth
Sunday after Trinity, Jesus, my beloved Saviour : for
soprano-, alto-, tenor-, bass-solo and chorus / Joh. Seb.
Bach ; English version by J. Michael Diack ; Klavierauszug
von Gunter Raphael. -- Leipzig : Breitkopf & Härtel, [1957],
c1933.
    1 vocal score (37 p.,) ; 27 cm. -- (Kirchenkantaten / Joh.
Seb. Bach ; Klavierauszüge ; Nr. 78)

    Caption title.
    Pl. no.: J.S.B.I.78.

    I. Diack, J. Michael (John Michael), 1869-1946. II.
Raphael, Gunter, 1903-1960. III. Title: Jesu, der du meine
Seele. IV. Title: Jesus, my beloved Saviour. V. Series:
Bach, Johann Sebastian, 1685-1750. Cantatas. Vocal scores.
Selections (1933) ; Nr. 78.

The caption is chosen as chief source of information in this case because it provides fuller information than the cover of the "list" title page. The date of publication "1957" is estimated from the Lizenz Nummer in the colophon.

Main entry is under the heading for Bach as composer with added entries required for Diack as translator and Raphael as arranger. The series added entry assigns a collective uniform title to the body of Bach's works represented by this particular series.

The uniform title of this work is based on *Jesu, der du meine Seele*, which is presumed to be the later, better known German language title because it is used to identify the work in the Schmieder thematic catalog of Bach's works. The modifier "Cantata" is added parenthetically because there are also three chorales and one chorale prelude by J.S. Bach with the same title as this cantata. The manifestation is identified in the uniform title by the specific material designation "Vocal score" and by the addition of the languages.

Edition Eulenburg

SYMPHONY No. 1

C minor

for Orchestra

by

JOHANNES BRAHMS

Op. 68

Foreword by Wilh. Altmann

Ernst Eulenburg Ltd., London · Ernst Eulenburg & Co. GmbH, Mainz

Edition Eulenburg GmbH, Zürich · Edition Eulenburg Inc., New York

(foreward: vii p.; miniature score:
166 p.; 19 cm; on p.[i] : facsimile
of autograph of opening theme in
4th movement)

Symphony, No. 1

I

Johannes Brahms, Op. 68
1833-1897

poco sostenuto

f legato

f legato

f legato

f legato

II.IV. Hörner in Es

2 Trompeten in C

Pauken in C-G

f

Violine I

f espress. e legato

Violine II

f espress. e legato

Bratsche

f espress. e legato

Violoncell

f espress. e legato

Kontrabaß

f pesante

No 425

E. E 4558   Ernst Eulenburg Ltd., London- Zürich

```
Brahms, Johannes, 1833-1897.
   [Symphonies, no. 1, op. 68, C minor]
   Symphony no. 1, C minor, for orchestra, op. 68 / by Johannes
Brahms ; foreword by Wilh. Altmann. -- London : Eulenburg ;
New York : Edition Eulenburg, [19--].
   1 miniature score (vii, 166 p.) : facsim. ; 19 cm.

   Publisher's no.: Edition Eulenburg no. 425.
   Pl. no: E.E. 4558.
```

Once again the title proper contains all of the title information because *Symphony* is the name of a type of composition. Both the London and New York publishers are included by virtue of a general Library of Congress rule interpretation for rule 1.4B8 (cf. Cataloging Service Bulletin 18). [19--] is the safest estimate of the date of publication that can be made in this case. Note that both publisher's and plate numbers are transcribed.

Main entry is under the heading for Brahms as composer. An added entry could be made for Altmann if desired, although because he contributed nothing to the musical content of the item, it is not required.

The uniform title is straightforward and comparable to the Mozart example above, although in this case the serial and opus numbers are used as distinguishing elements.

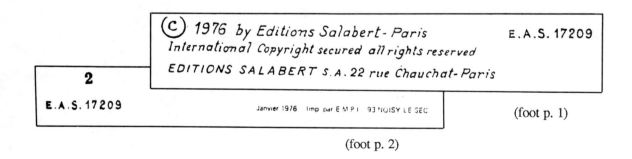

ERIK SATIE
CHEZ LE DOCTEUR

PIANO et CHANT

EDITIONS SALABERT

22, rue Chauchat - PARIS

575 Madison Avenue and 57th Street - NEW YORK

Printed in France

© 1976 by Editions Salabert - Paris   E.A.S. 17209
International Copyright secured all rights reserved
EDITIONS SALABERT S.A. 22 rue Chauchat - Paris

2

E.A.S. 17209   Janvier 1976   Imp par E M P I 93 NOISY LE SEC   (foot p. 1)

(foot p. 2)

(3 p., 32 cm.; in caption: Paroles de Vincent Hyspa; the melody ranges from C to D^1)

```
Satie, Erik, 1866-1925.
   Chez le docteur : piano et chant / Erik Satie ; [paroles de
Vincent Hyspa]. -- Paris ; New York : Editions Salabert,
c1976.
   1 score (3 p.) ; 32 cm.

For medium voice and piano.
Pl. no.: E.A.S. 17209.

   I. Hyspa, Vincent, 1865-1938.   II. Title.
```

The name of the author of the words is interpolated into the statement of responsibility because it appears prominently in the caption. The copyright date is transcribed from the bottom of the first page of music.

Main entry is under Satie as composer. Hyspa, the author of the words, requires an added entry.

There is no uniform title displayed in the bibliographic record for this item because the title proper of the item is identical with the uniform title for the work, *Chez le docteur*.

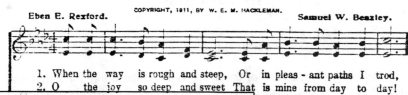

GOSPEL BELLS

A
CHOICE COLLECTION
of

Gospel Songs and Standard Hymns

for

Church, Sunday School, Endeavor and Evangelist

Edited by
E. O. EXCELL AND W. E. M. HACKLEMAN

PRICE LIST

Binding	Per Copy, Postpaid	Per Dozen, Not Prepaid	Per 100, Not Prepaid
Flexible	25c	$2 00	$15 00
Board	30c	2 50	20 00
Cloth	35c	3 00	25 00

Published by

CHRISTIAN BOARD OF PUBLICATION	HACKLEMAN MUSIC COMPANY
2712-2716 Pine Street	416-419 Majestic Building
ST. LOUIS, MO.	INDIANAPOLIS, IND.

(256 p.; 20 cm.; "Index, titles in Roman, first lines in italics, p. 254-256)

Gospel bells : a choice collection of gospel songs and
    standard hymns for church, Sunday school, endeavor, and
evangelist / edited by E.O. Excell and W.E.M. Hackleman.
-- St. Louis, Mo. : Christian Board of Publication ;
Indianapolis, Ind. : Hackleman Music Co., [191-?]

    1 close score (256 p.) ; 20 cm.

    Index of titles and first lines: p. 254-256.

    I. Excell, E. O. (Edwin Othello), 1851-1921.
II. Hackleman, W. E. M.

Both publisher's names are transcribed in this example because it is likely that the two companies performed different functions in the publication process. The item is described as "1 close score" because the separate vocal parts are written on two staves throughout.

Main entry is under title because the authorship is diverse. Added entries are required for both editors (i.e., compilers).

THE THEATRE GUILD

presents

OKLAHOMA!

A Musical Play

Based on the play
"GREEN GROW THE LILACS" by Lynn Riggs

Music by

RICHARD RODGERS

Book and Lyrics by

OSCAR HAMMERSTEIN, 2nd

Production directed by ROUBEN MAMOULIAN

Production under the supervision of
Theresa Helburn and Lawrence Langner

Musical Director	*Costumes by*	*Settings by*
JAY S. BLACKTON	MILES WHITE	LEMUEL AYERS

Dances by AGNES DE MILLE

Orchestrations by RUSSELL BENNETT

Price, $12.00

VOCAL SCORE

(Edited by ALBERT SIRMAY)

(208 p.; 30 cm.; lower left corner each page: C-523-; at foot of first page of music: Williamson Music Inc., New York, N.Y. DeSylva, Brown & Henderson Inc., Sole Selling Agent)

```
Rodgers, Richard, 1902-
   [Oklahoma! Vocal score]
   The Theatre Guild presents Oklahoma! : a musical play based
on the play "Green grow the lilacs" by Lynn Riggs / music by
Richard Rodgers ; book and lyrics by Oscar Hammerstein, 2nd
... ; vocal score edited by Albert Sirmay. -- New York, N.Y.
: Williamson Music : sole selling agent, DeSylva, Brown &
Henderson, c1943.
   1 vocal score (208 p.) ; 30 cm.

   Pl. no.: C-523-.

   I. Hammerstein, Oscar, 1895-1960.  II. Sirmay, Albert.  III.
Riggs, Lynn, 1899-    Green grow the lilacs.  IV. Title.
V. Title: Oklahoma!
```

Note that the title proper includes the words that precede the actual title *Oklahoma!* on the title page. The statements of responsibility that pertain to the staged production but not to this item have not been transcribed, and the omission is indicated with an ellipsis. The price is not included because it is not current.

Main entry is under the heading for Rodgers, who wrote the music. Added entries are required for Hammerstein who wrote the lyrics, for Sirmay who arranged this version for piano, and for the Riggs book on which the present work was based. A separate title added entry is provided for *Oklahoma!* to provide direct access to the title of the work.

The uniform title is based on the original and currently best known title of the musical work and includes an indication of the present physical manifestation "vocal score." Language is not included because no translation is present.

(verso rear cover)

RAGTIME

MAIN TITLE
NEWSREEL
I COULD LOVE A MILLION GIRLS
TRAIN RIDE
TATEH'S PICTURE BOOK
LOWER EAST SIDE
DELMONICO POLKA
COALHOUSE AND SARAH
WALTZ FOR EVELYN
ONE MORE HOUR

SARAH'S RESPONSIBILITY
CHANGE YOUR WAY
CLEF CLUB No. 1
ATLANTIC CITY
CLEF CLUB No. 2
SARAH'S FUNERAL
DÉNOUEMENT
(STAND UP FOR JESUS)
MORGAN LIBRARY TAKEOVER
RHINELANDER WALDO
COALHOUSE'S PRAYER
RAGTIME

DINO DE LAURENTIIS PRESENTS A MILOS FORMAN FILM
"RAGTIME" Starring JAMES CAGNEY   Music by RANDY NEWMAN
A SUNLEY PRODUCTION   Executive Producers MICHAEL HAUSMAN
and BERNARD WILLIAMS   Screenplay by MICHAEL WELLER
From the Novel "Ragtime" by E.L. DOCTOROW
Produced by DINO DE LAURENTIIS   Directed by MILOS FORMAN
A PARAMOUNT RELEASE

Columbia Pictures Publications

PO396SMX   PIANO/VOCAL/CHORDS $7.95

ISBN: 0-89898-114-X

© 1981 WIDE MUSIC INC.

(title page)

Newman, Randy.
   [Ragtime. Vocal score. Selections]
   Ragtime / [music by Randy Newman]. - - [United States :
Columbia Pictures Publications], c1981.
   1 vocal score (64 p.) : ports. ; 31 cm.

   Original music from the motion picture arr. for piano;
includes chord symbols.
   Contents: Main title -- Newsreel -- I could love a million
girls -- Train ride -- Tateh's picture book -- Lower East
Side -- Delmonico polka -- Coalhouse and Sarah -- Waltz for
Evelyn -- One more hour -- Sarah's responsibility -- Change
your way -- Clef Club no. 1 -- Atlantic City -- Clef Club
no. 2 -- Sarah's funeral -- Denouement : Stand up for Jesus
-- Morgan Library take-over -- Rhinelander Waldo
-- Coalhouse's prayer -- Ragtime.
   Publisher's no.: P03966SMX.
   ISBN 0-89898-114-X (pbk.) ; $7.95.

   I. Ragtime (Motion picture).

This example requires some creative interpretation of the rules because the title page presents only the title proper and all the remaining details of publication are scattered throughout the item. Because the composer's name is displayed prominently in the caption of each musical excerpt, it is interpolated into the statement of responsibility. Although most of this music is not vocal music, the term "vocal score" is the best specific material designation because the original music was orchestral, and because "piano score," the other alternative, would be more misleading. Note the "E♭" above the stave is described as a "chord symbol."

   Main entry is under the heading for Newman, the composer. A uniform title is required to indicate the altered physical manifestation "vocal score." The term "Selections" is added, because only the featured tunes are included in this collection; the background, or incidental music is not included. An added entry for the motion picture, as related work, is required and takes the form of a uniform title heading. However, the title proper is not traced because it would be meaningless alone. (cf. MCD 21.30J).

(top of p. 10, first page of music; each subsequent caption has the same statement of responsibility)

(p. 1-8 contain portraits of the characters from the motion picture; music p. 10-64 with scenes from the motion picture interspersed; music mostly for piano, with some vocals; 31 cm.)

(table of contents, p. [3])

(title page)

Neil Young

Hawks & Doves

Exclusive Selling Agent for
the United States and Canada
WARNER BROS. PUBLICATIONS INC.
75 Rockefeller Plaza • New York, NY 10019

$7.95
in U.S.A.

(verso rear cover)

SILVER FIDDLE

VF0842

114

Young, Neil.
    Hawkes & Doves / Neil Young. -- [United States] : Silver
Fiddle ; New York, N.Y. : exclusive selling agent Warner
Bros. Publications, c1981.
    1 score (55 p.) ; 30 cm.

    Songs from the record album of the same title; for voice
and piano with chord symbols and guitar chord diagrams;
words printed also as text.
    Contents: Little wing -- The old homestead -- Lost in
space -- Capt. Kennedy -- Stayin' power -- Coastline
-- Union man -- Comin' apart at every nail -- Hawks & Doves.
    Publisher's no.: Vf0842.

    I. Title.

    This example is also more like a sound recording than a score. In fact, it is what is referred to as a "pop-folio" and is really a printed manifestation of a sound recording. Note the description includes the term "guitar chord diagrams" as well as "chord symbols."
    The Library of Congress does not often distribute cataloging for this type of material. When they do, they have traditionally not included uniform titles in those descriptions. It is likely that a library that owned both this folio and the original recording would profit from the use of uniform titles to avoid confusion in an integrated catalog. In that case, "Hawks & Doves. Vocal score" would be appropriate.

(*Phonolog* lists an album; *Hawks & Doves* (Reprise HS 2297); 55 pages; no illustrations; 30 cm.)

WELCOME TO THE REAL WORLD

(title page)

WARNER BROS. PUBLICATIONS INC.
265 Secaucus Road • Secaucus, N.J. 07094
A Warner Communications Company

$9.95
in U.S.A.

VF1272

(rear cover)

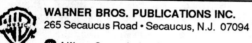

(first page of music)

BROKEN WINGS

Words and Music by
RICHARD PAGE, STEVE GEORGE
and JOHN LANG

Medium Fast Rock

G♯sus2

mp

(48 p. ; 31 cm., photos on p. 2-4)

Welcome to the real world / Mr. Mister. -- Secaucus, N.J.
    (265 Secaucus Rd., Secaucus, N.J. 07094) : Warner-
Tamerlane Pub. Corp., c1986.
    1 score (48 p.) : ill. ; 31 cm.

    Rock music, as recorded by the musical group Mr. Mister;
voice and keyboard with chord symbols and guitar chord
diagrams.
    Words and music by Richard Page, Steve George, John Lang,
Steve Farris, and Pat Mosteletto.
    Contents: Broken wings -- Welcome to the real world -- Kyrie
eleison -- Is it love -- Uniform of youth -- Run to her
-- Into my own hands -- Tangent tears -- Don't slow down
-- Black/white.
    Publisher's no.: VF1272.

    I. Page, Richard.   II. Mr. Mister (Musical group).   III.
Title.

This is another pop-folio, though in this case the music is not written by any one performer, but by all the members of the group in various combinations. The statement of responsibility includes the name of the group, as it appears in the chief source, thus mirroring the description of the corresponding sound recording.

Because this is a collection, and because authorship is diverse, main entry is under title. Following rule 21.6C2, an added entry is made under the heading for the first named contributor (Page's name appears first in each listing). An added entry is made for the performing group as a related body (cf. 21.30F).

(recto container)

(Program notes appear on the verso of the container)

TMK(S) ® by RCA Corporation
© 1967, RCA Records, New York, NY • Printed in USA

Timings: Side 1 - 16:06 • Side 2 - 15:43
Library of Congress card number: R67-3339
Cover painting by Barron Storey

(Recorded March 8, 1954)

(verso container)

Side **1** Stereo
VICS 1265 (UVRS-1467)

Strauss

Also sprach Zarathustra, Op. 30
Part 1

Chicago Symphony Orchestra
Fritz Reiner, Conductor

TWK ®© REGISTERED • MARCA (©) REGISTRADA(©)
RADIO CORPORATION OF AMERICA-MADE IN U.S.A.

Side **2** Stereo
VICS 1265 (UVRS-1468)

Strauss

Also sprach Zarathustra, Op. 30
Concluded

Chicago Symphony Orchestra
Fritz Reiner, Conductor
John Weicher, *Violinist*

TWK ®© REGISTERED • MARCA (©) REGISTRADA(©)
RADIO CORPORATION OF AMERICA-MADE IN U.S.A.

```
Strauss, Richard, 1864-1949.
    Also sprach Zarathustra [sound recording] : op. 30 /
Strauss. -- New York, N.Y. : RCA Victrola, c1967.
    1 sound disc (32 min.) : analog, 33 1/3 rpm, stereo. ; 12
in. -- (Immortal performances)

    RCA Victrola: VICS 1265.
    Symphonic poem.
    Chicago Symphony Orchestra ; Fritz Reiner, conductor.
    Recorded Mar. 8, 1954.

    I. Reiner, Fritz, 1888-1963.  II. Chicago Symphony
Orchestra.  III. Title.  IV. Series.
```

The labels are the chief source of information for this analog sound disc. Because the title is not the name of a type of composition, the opus number is transcribed as other title information. The label name, "RCA Victrola," is given instead of the publisher's name. The durations are added together for the "extent of item" aspect of the physical description area. The label name and manufacturer's serial number are given as the first note. Other notes describe the work, give statements of responsibility for the performance (not included in area 1 because this is not the type of music in which the contribution of the performers goes beyond execution), and give information on the recording session. Notice that in the statement of responsibility note, names of persons or bodies performing different functions are separated by a space-semi-colon-space. The notes that appear on the verso of the container are minor, so they are not noted in the description.

Main entry is under the heading for Strauss, the composer, with added entries for the performers.

Because the composer's original title, *Also sprach Zarathustra*, is identical with the title proper, no uniform title is displayed in the bibliographic record.

BURBANK, HOME OF WARNER BROS. RECORDS

AMERICA

Produced by Ian Samwell with Jeff Dexter,
and America
Engineered by Ken Scott

BS 2576
(S39997)RE1

1. RIVERSIDE (Bunnell) 3:02
2. SANDMAN (Bunnell) 5:03
3. THREE ROSES (Bunnell) 3:56
4. CHILDREN (Bunnell) 3:07
5. A HORSE WITH NO NAME 4:10
   (Bunnell)
6. HERE (Beckley) 5:30

STEREO

Warner Bros. Inc. · 3300 Warner Blvd., Burbank, Calif. 91505 · a Warner Co.

BURBANK, HOME OF WARNER BROS. RECORDS

AMERICA

Produced by Ian Samwell with Jeff Dexter,
and America
Engineered by Ken Scott

BS 2576
(S39998)

SIDE
2

1. I NEED YOU (Beckley) 3:04
2. RAINY DAY (Peek) 3:00
3. NEVER FOUND THE TIME (Peek) 3:50
4. CLARICE (Beckley) 4:00
5. DONKEY JAW (Peek) 5:17
6. PIGEON SONG (Bunnell) 2:17

STEREO

Warner Bros. Inc. · 3300 Warner Blvd., Burbank, Calif. 91505 · a Warner Communications Company.

A HORSE WITH NO NAME (Bunnell) (4:10)
HERE (Beckley) (5:30)

NEVER FOUND THE TIME
CLARICE
DONKEY JAW
PIGEON SONG (Bunnell) (2:17)

All selections Warner Bros. Music Corp. (ASCAP)
AMERICA is Dewey Bunnell, Gerry Beckley and Dan Peek
Produced by Ian Samwell with Jeff Dexter and AMERICA
Engineered by Ken Scott
Recorded at Trident Studios, London, England
"A Horse with No Name" recorded at Morgan Studios, London
Cover Photos and Design by Nigel Waymouth
Logo Flash Fox

Warner Bros. Records Inc., a Subsidiary & Licensee of Warner Bros. Inc., 4000 Warner Blvd., Burbank, Calif. 91505
44 East 50th Street, New York, New York 10022 · Made in U.S.A. ℗ 1971 Warner Bros. Records Inc.

(on edge of container: ℗ 1972)

America (Musical group).
    America [sound recording]. -- Burbank, Calif. : Warner Bros.
Records, p1972.
    1 sound disc (51 min.) : analog, 33 1/3 rpm, stereo. ; 12
in.

    Warner Bros. Records: BS 2576.
    Songs written and performed by America.
    Recorded in London.
    Contents: Riverside (3:02) ; Sandman (5:03) ; Three roses
(3:54) ; Children (3:07) ; A horse with no name (4:10) /
Bunnell -- Here (6:00) ; I need you (3:04) / Beckley
-- Rainy day (3:00) ; Never found the time (3:50) / Peek
-- Clarice / Beckley (4:00) -- Donkey jaw / Peek (6:00)
-- Pigeon song / Bunnell (2:17).

    I. Bunnell, Dewey. Songs. Selections II. Beckley, Gerry.
Songs Selections. III. Peek, Dan. Songs. Selections.
IV. Title.

The labels again provide the chief source of information. Note that the title proper consists solely of the name of the performing group. Note also that the durations of the individual selections are recorded in the contents note.

Because the songs are composed individually by the three members of the performing group, this recording is considered a collection. Main entry is under the heading for America, as principal performer. Added entries in the form of composer-collective uniform title analytics are stipulated by RI 21.7B9(g) because there are three or more titles for each composer.

(A four page pamphlet with song texts and photographs of Queen is included in the container. On bottom of verso of container: " ... recorded at Trident, Wessex, Rockfield and Air Studios ... composed, arranged and performed exclusively by Queen ... ℗, ©, 1974 Elektra/Asylum/Nonesuch Records ... Los Angeles, California ... .")

Queen (Musical group).
    Sheer heart attack [sound recording] / [composed, arranged and performed exclusively by] Queen. -- Los Angeles, Calif. : Elektra, p1974.
    1 sound disc (40 min.) : analog, 33 1/3 rpm, stereo. ; 12 in.

    Elektra: 7E-1026.
    Rock music.
    Recorded at Trident, Wessex, Rockfield and Air Studios.
    Song texts ([4] p. : ill.) in container.
    Contents: Brighten Rock (6:00) -- Killer Queen (3:00) -- Tenement funster! (2:48) -- Flick of the wrist (3:18) -- Lily of the valley (1:41) -- Now I'm here (4:15) -- In the lap of the gods (3:23) -- Stone cold crazy (2:14) -- Dear friends (1:07) -- Misfire (1:58) -- Bring back that Leroy Brown (2:17) -- She makes me : stormtrooper in stilettoes (4:10) -- In the lap of the gods -- Revisited (3:23).

    I. Title.

In this example the performing group is represented as collective composer as well as a performer whose contribution goes beyond mere execution. Thus, its name is transcribed in the statement of responsibility area. It has been chosen as main entry, because its contribution is that of principal performer.

123

(bio-bibliographical program notes on verso container)

```
Bizet, Georges, 1838-1875.
   [Selections]
   Carmen suite : no. 1 ; Jeux d'enfantes ; L'Arlésienne :
suite no. 1 [sound recording] / Bizet. -- [Los Angeles,
Calif.] : Angel, p1973.
   1 sound disc (44 min.) : analog, 33 1/3 rpm, stereo. ; 12
in.

   Angel: S-36955.
   Opera excerpts (1st work) ; the 2nd work originally for
piano, 4 hands, orchestrated by the composer ; the 3rd work
taken from the incidental music for the play by Alphonse
Daudet, arr. by the composer.
   Orchestre de Paris ; Daniel Barenboim, conductor.
   Recorded in France.
   Program notes on container.
   Durations: 11:45; 11:57; 19:35.

   I. Barenboim, Daniel, 1942-      II. Orchestre de Paris.
III. Bizet, Georges, 1838-1875. Carmen. Selections.  IV.
Bizet, Georges, 1838-1875. Jeux d'enfants. Selections;
arr. V. Bizet, Georges, 1838-1875. Arlésienne. Suite.
VI. Title.  VII. Title: Jeux d'enfants. VIII. Title:
Arlésienne.
```

Because the container provides no collective title for this recording, the labels are used as chief source of information. The titles are transcribed accordingly. Because the works are all by one person, the general material designation precedes the statement of responsibility. Because this is art music, the performer's names are not included in the original statement of responsibility, but are given in a note. The place of publication is supplied by the cataloger. The durations of the individual works are given in a single note, because the collective title paragraph eliminates the need for a contents note.

Main entry is under the heading for Bizet as composer. Added entries are required for the performers.

The collective uniform title "Selections" is chosen to represent the diversity of the works contained on this recording. Analytical added entries are provided for each of the individual works.

(program notes on verso container)

Wagner: Wesendonk Lieder
1. Der Engel • 2. Stehe still!
3. Im Treibhaus • 4. Schmerzen • 5. Traume

JANET BAKER (mezzo soprano)
LONDON PHILHARMONIC ORCHESTRA,
SIR ADRIAN BOULT

RL-1-32017
(SQ-1-37199)
STEREO
33-1/3
Recorded in England
℗1976 EMI Records Limited

Richard Strauss:
1. Liebeshymnus • 2. Ruhe, meine Seele!
3. Das Rosenband • 4. Muttertändelei
Brahms: 5. Alto Rhapsody, Op. 53

JANET BAKER (mezzo soprano)
LONDON PHILHARMONIC ORCHESTRA,
SIR ADRIAN BOULT cond.
5. With the John Alldis Choir

RL-2-32017
(SQ-2-37199)
STEREO
33-1/3
Recorded in England
℗1976 1971 EMI Records Limited

Janet Baker

BRAHMS: ALTO RHAPSODY
WAGNER: WESENDONK LIEDER
STRAUSS: FOUR SONGS

SIR ADRIAN BOULT
London Philharmonic Orchestra
*The John Alldis Choir

Enclosed: German texts & English translation

(container)

126

```
Baker, Janet.
    Janet Baker [sound recording]. -- [Los Angeles, Calif.] :
Angel, p1976.
    1 sound disc (47 min.) : analog, 33 1/3 rpm, quad., SQ ; 12
in.

        Angel: RL-32017 (SQ 37199).
        Title from container.
        Janet Baker, mezzo-soprano ; London Philharmonic Orchestra ;
    Sir Adrian Boult, conductor ; The John Alldis Choir.
        Song texts in German with English translations ([4] p. ; 28
    cm.) inserted.
        Contents: Wesendonk Lieder / Wagner ; texts by Mathilde
    Wesendonk (22:59) -- Liebeshymnus : op. 32, no. 3 (1:59) ;
    Ruhe, meine Seele : op. 27, no. 1 (4:26) / Richard Strauss ;
    Klopstock (3:26) -- Muttertändelei : op. 43, no. 2 / Richard
    Strauss ; Burger (2:11) -- Rhapsody for contralto, male
    chorus and orchestra, op. 53 / Brahms ; Goethe (11:40).

        I. Boult, Adrian, Sir, 1889-      II. London Philharmonic
    Orchestra. III. John Alldis Choir.  IV. Wagner, Richard,
    1813-1883.  Wesendonk-Lieder; arr.  V. Strauss, Richard,
    1864-1949.  Lieder, op. 32.  Liebeshymnus; arr.  VI.
    Strauss, Richard, 1864-1949.  Lieder, op. 27.  Ruhe, meine
    Seele; arr.  VII. Strauss, Richard, 1864-1949. Lieder, op.
    36.  Roenband; arr. VIII. Strauss, Richard, 1864-1949.
    Gesange, op. 43.  Muttertändelei; arr.  IX. Brahms,
    Johannes, 1833-1897.  Rhapsodies, alto, men's voices,
    orchestra, op. 53.  X. Title.
```

In this case the performer's name as presented on the container constitutes a collective title for the recording that is not provided by the labels, so the container is used as chief source of information.

Main entry is under the heading for Janet Baker as principal performer. Composer-uniform title analytical added entries have been provided for each of the works performed, though this recording would fall into the class of so-called "recital" recordings that the Library of Congress would not analyze (cf. RI 21.7B); therefore, these analytical entries are optional. Note that the Wagner work uses a later, better known title as uniform title (Wagner's title was *Gedichte für eine Frauenstimme*).

(45 rpm. ; 7 in.)

"DEDICATED TO
TO THE ONE I LOVE"
(Lowman Pauling, Ralph Bass)

STX-1026
STX-1026-A
Trousdale
Music,
BMI
Time: 3:
(Intro. 0:
℗ 197
STAX Rec

THE TEMPREES
Produced by Jo Bridges & Tom Nixon
Arranged by Lester Snell
& Tom Nixon

DISTRIBUTED BY

KELEY, CALIFOR

"EXPLAIN IT TO HER MAMA"
(Cleophus Fultz & Leon Moore)

STX-1026
STX-1026-B
Stripe Music,
East/
Memphis
Music, BMI
Time: 2:57
(Intro. 0:08)
℗ 1977
STAX Records

THE TEMPREES
Produced & Arranged by
Jo Bridges & Tom Nixon
Rhythm by
We Produced Band

DISTRIBUTED BY FANTASY RECORDS, BERKELEY, CALIFORNIA

Double HITTERS

(paper sleeve)

Temprees (Musical group).
 Dedicated to the one I love / Lowman Pauling, Ralph Bass ;
[performed by] The Temprees ; arr. by Lester Snell & Tom
Nixon. Explain it to her Mama / Cleophus Fultz & Leon Moore
; arr. by Jo Bridges & Tom Nixon ; [performed by] The
Temprees ; rhythm by We Produced Band [sound recording].
-- [United States] : Stax Records ; Berkeley, Calif. :
distributed by Fantasy Records, p1977.
 1 sound disc (7 min.) : analog, 45 rpm ; 7 in. -- (Double
hitter)

 Stax: STX-1026.
 Soul music.
 Durations: 3:32; 2:57.

 I. Pauling, Lowman. II. Bass, Ralph. III. Snell, Lester.
IV. Nixon, Tom. V. Fultz, Cleophus. VI. Moore, Leon. VII.
Bridges, Jo. VIII. We Produced Band. IX. Title. X. Title:
Explain it to her Mama.

This 45 rpm recording illustrates the difficulties of transcription and the potential complexity of entry for popular music recordings. Note the recurrence of the statement of responsibility for the performing group, which appears in conjunction with each title on each label. Note also, that because authorship is diverse, the general material designation follows the entire title and statement of responsibility area.

Main entry is under heading for the group as principal performer, because this recording is a collection without a collective title, and because the music is of the type in which the participation of the performers goes beyond execution. Added entries are required for the composers of the music and the authors of the words. Because these functions are not readily apparent from the item, and because there is little or no information to be found in reference sources, entries are provided for all of the names given. Note that even though certain persons are indentified as "arrangers," this music is not "arranged" in the traditional sense. In popular music, the term "arranged" means "scored," or, more traditionally, "orchestrated."

"This album ... is Mother Maybelle Carter ... playing guitar and autoharp.... Larry Butler, Producer." (from liner notes in center of album cover)

MOTHER MAYBELLE CARTER

KG 32436
C 32437
STEREO

SIDE 1
AL 32437
℗ 1973 CBS, Inc.

1. DIALOGUE - 1st Record 1927 - Original Carter Family 2:00
2. GOOD OLD MOUNTAIN DEW 1:59
   - S.Wiseman - B. Lunsford-
3. STILL 3:17 - B. Anderson-
4. ARKANSAS TRAVELLER 4:52
   - -Arr. M. Carter - With Dialogue
5. WATERLOO 2:00
   - M. Wilkin - J. Loudermilk -
6. BLACK MOUNTAIN RAG 1:48
   - Arr. M. Carter -

MOTHER MAYBELLE CARTER

KG 32436
C 32437
STEREO

SIDE 2
BL 32437
℗ 1973 CBS, Inc.

1. DIALOGUE - JIMMY ROGERS & TRAIN 1:29
2. WABASH CANNONBALL 2:06 - A.P. Carter -
3. ROCKY TOP 3:04 - F. Bryant - B. Bryant -
4. RELEASE ME 2:37
   - E. Miller - W.S. Stevenson - R. Yount -
5. HEY LIBERTY 2:17 - Arr. M. Carter -
6. CHINESE BREAKDOWN 5:32
   - Arr. M. Carter -
   With Dialogue

MOTHER MAYBELLE CARTER

KG 32436
C 32438
STEREO

SIDE 3
AL 3243
℗ 1973 CBS,

1. THE BELLS OF ST. MARY 3:17 - E. Adams -
   D. Furber - With Dialogue
2. THE WORLD NEEDS A MELODY 3:11
   - R. Lane - L. Henley - J. Slate -
3. NEVER ON SUNDAY 3:39
   - B. Towne - M. Hadjidakis -
4. TENNESSEE WALTZ 3:20
   - P. King - R. Stewart -
5. RED WING 3:41
   - Arr. M. Carter -
   With Dialogue

MOTHER MAYBELLE CARTER

KG 32436
C 32438
STEREO

SIDE 4
AL 32438
℗ 1973 CBS, Inc.

1. WILDWOOD FLOWER 5:46 - A. P. Carter -
   With Dialogue
2. RUNNING BEAR 3:06 - J. T. Richardson -
3. DRUNKARD'S HELL 4:05 - Arr. M. Carter -
4. SWEET ALLIE LEE 3:33
   - -Arr. M. Carter -

Carter, Mother Maybelle.
    Mother Maybelle Carter [sound recording]. -- New York :
Columbia, p1973.
    2 sound discs (67 min.) : analog, 33 1/3 rpm, stereo. ; 12
in.

    Columbia: KG 32346 (32437-32438).
    Mother Maybelle Carter, guitar or autoharp with instrumental
ensemble; with spoken reminiscences.
    Contents: Dialogue : 1st record 1927 / original Carter
family (2:00) -- Good old mountain dew / S. Wiseman, B
Lunsford (1:59) -- Still / B. Anderson (3:17) -- Arkansas
traveller / arr. M. Carter ; with dialogue (4:52)
-- Waterloo / M. Wilkin, J. Loudermilk (2:00) -- Black
Mountain rag / arr. M. Carter (1:48) -- Dialogue / Jimmy
Rogers & Train (1:29) -- Wabash Canonball / A.P. Carter
(2:06) -- Rocky Top / F. Bryant, B. Bryant (3:04) -- Release
me / E. Miller, W.S. Stevenson, R. Yount (2:37) -- Hey
Liberty / arr. M. Carter (2:17) -- Chinese breakdown / arr.
M. Carter ; with dialogue (5:32) -- The bells of St. Mary /
E. Adams, D. Furber ; with dialogue (3:17) -- The world
needs a melody / R. Lane, L. Henley, J. Slate (3:11)
-- Never on Sunday / B. Towne, M. Hadjidakis (3:39)
-- Tennessee waltz / P. King, R. Stewart (3:20) -- Red wing
/ arr. M. Carter ; with dialogue (3:41) -- Wildwood flower /
A.P. Carter ; with dialogue (5:46) -- Running bear / J.T.
Richardson (3:06) -- Drunkard's hell / arr. M. Carter
(4:05) -- Sweet Allie Lee / arr. M. Carter (3:33)

    I. Title.

    This example is similar to the Janet Baker example above, except that this is a recording of music in a
popular idiom. Main entry is under the heading for Carter as principal performer; analysis is not provided because
this is not art music. Note once again the use of the term "arranged" in the popular idiom to indicate "orchestrated."

(recto container)

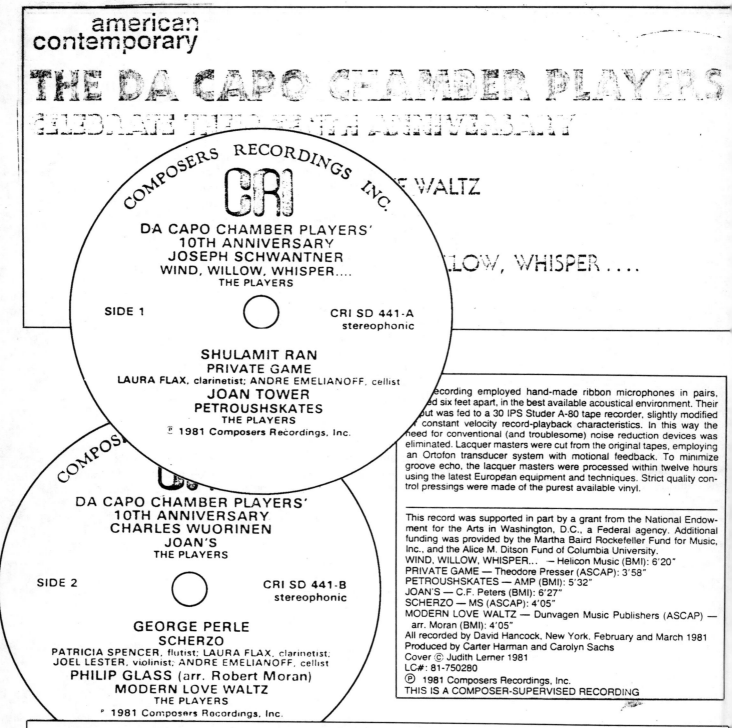

american
contemporary

THE DA CAPO CHAMBER PLAYERS

CELEBRATE THEIR 10TH ANNIVERSARY

COMPOSERS RECORDINGS INC.

CRI

DA CAPO CHAMBER PLAYERS'
10TH ANNIVERSARY
JOSEPH SCHWANTNER
WIND, WILLOW, WHISPER....
THE PLAYERS

SIDE 1   CRI SD 441-A
                         stereophonic

SHULAMIT RAN
PRIVATE GAME
LAURA FLAX, clarinetist; ANDRE EMELIANOFF, cellist
JOAN TOWER
PETROUSHSKATES
THE PLAYERS
℗ 1981 Composers Recordings, Inc.

DA CAPO CHAMBER PLAYERS'
10TH ANNIVERSARY
CHARLES WUORINEN
JOAN'S
THE PLAYERS

SIDE 2   CRI SD 441-B
                         stereophonic

GEORGE PERLE
SCHERZO
PATRICIA SPENCER, flutist; LAURA FLAX, clarinetist;
JOEL LESTER, violinist; ANDRE EMELIANOFF, cellist
PHILIP GLASS (arr. Robert Moran)
MODERN LOVE WALTZ
THE PLAYERS
℗ 1981 Composers Recordings, Inc.

recording employed hand-made ribbon microphones in pairs,
ed six feet apart, in the best available acoustical environment. Their
ut was fed to a 30 IPS Studer A-80 tape recorder, slightly modified
constant velocity record-playback characteristics. In this way the
eed for conventional (and troublesome) noise reduction devices was
eliminated. Lacquer masters were cut from the original tapes, employing
an Ortofon transducer system with motional feedback. To minimize
groove echo, the lacquer masters were processed within twelve hours
using the latest European equipment and techniques. Strict quality con-
trol pressings were made of the purest available vinyl.

This record was supported in part by a grant from the National Endow-
ment for the Arts in Washington, D.C., a Federal agency. Additional
funding was provided by the Martha Baird Rockefeller Fund for Music,
Inc., and the Alice M. Ditson Fund of Columbia University.
WIND, WILLOW, WHISPER... — Helicon Music (BMI): 6'20"
PRIVATE GAME — Theodore Presser (ASCAP): 3'58"
PETROUSHSKATES — AMP (BMI): 5'32"
JOAN'S — C.F. Peters (BMI): 6'27"
SCHERZO — MS (ASCAP): 4'05"
MODERN LOVE WALTZ — Dunvagen Music Publishers (ASCAP) —
    arr. Moran (BMI): 4'05"
All recorded by David Hancock, New York, February and March 1981
Produced by Carter Harman and Carolyn Sachs
Cover © Judith Lerner 1981
LC#: 81-750280
℗ 1981 Composers Recordings, Inc.
THIS IS A COMPOSER-SUPERVISED RECORDING

THE DA CAPO CHAMBER PLAYERS' 10TH ANNIVERSARY CELEBRATION
Patricia Spencer, flutist; Laura Flax, clarinetist; Joel Lester, violinist; André Emelianoff, cellist;
Joan Tower, pianist

(verso container)

Da Capo Chamber Players.
    Da Capo Chamber Players' 10th anniversary
[sound recording]. -- [New York, N.Y.] : Composers
Recordings, p1981.
    1 sound disc (31 min.) : analog, 33 1/3 rpm, stereo. ;
12 in. -- (American contemporary)

    Composers Recordings: CRI SD 441.
    Titles on container: The Da Capo Chamber Players
celebrate their tenth anniversary ; The Da Capo Chamber
Players' 10th anniversary celebration.
    Editions recorded: Helicon Music; T. Presser; AMP; C.F.
Peters; ms.; Dunvagen.
    Recorded by David Hancock, New York, Feb. and Mar. 1981.
    Contents: Wind, willow, whisper / Jospeh Schwantner
(6:20) -- Private game / Shulamit Ran (3:58)
-- Petroushskates / Joan Tower (5:32) -- Joan's / Charles
Wuorinen (6:27) -- Scherzo / George Perle (4:05) -- Modern
love waltz / Philip Glass ; arr. Robert Moran (4:05).

    I. Schwantner, Joseph C. Wind, willow, whisper. II.
Ran, Shulamit, 1947-   Private game. III. Tower, Joan,
1938- Petroushskates. IV. Wuorinen, Charles. Joan's.
V. Perle, George, 1915-   Scherzo, instrumental ensemble.
VI. Glass, Philip. Modern love waltz; arr. VII. Title.
VIII. Title: Da Capo Chamber Players celebrate their 10th
anniversary. IX. Title: Da Capo Chamber Players' tenth
anniversary. X. Series.

In this example the collective title is transcribed from the label; alternative versions of the title, which appear on the container, are included in a note.

Main entry is under the heading for the performing ensemble as principal performer. Analytical added entries are provided for each of the compositions. Title added entries are made for each of the alternative collective titles.

(first offered for sale in 1978)

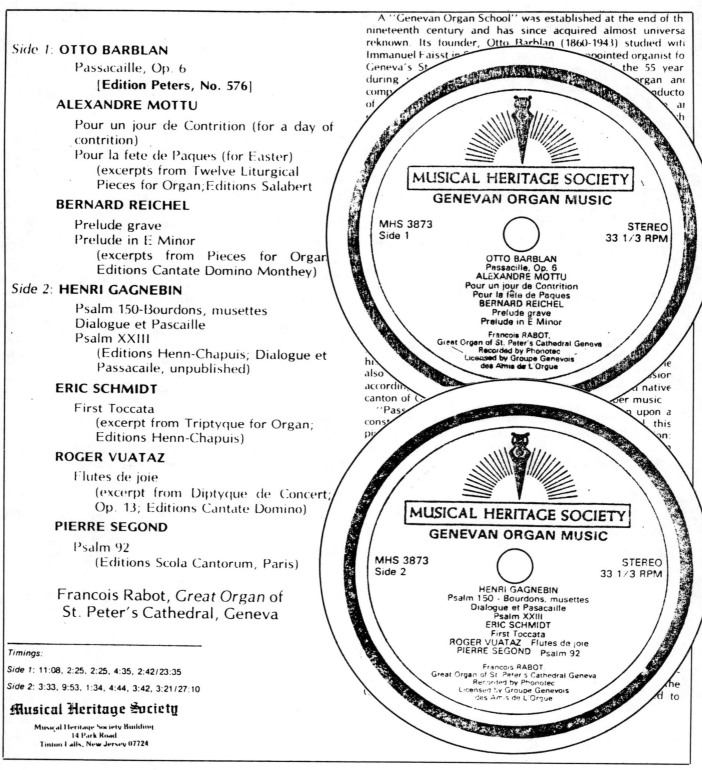

Side 1: **OTTO BARBLAN**

Passacaille, Op. 6
[Edition Peters, No. 576]

ALEXANDRE MOTTU

Pour un jour de Contrition (for a day of contrition)
Pour la fete de Paques (for Easter)
(excerpts from Twelve Liturgical Pieces for Organ; Editions Salabert

BERNARD REICHEL

Prelude grave
Prelude in E Minor
(excerpts from Pieces for Organ Editions Cantate Domino Monthey)

Side 2: **HENRI GAGNEBIN**

Psalm 150-Bourdons, musettes
Dialogue et Pascaille
Psalm XXIII
(Editions Henn-Chapuis; Dialogue et Passacaile, unpublished)

ERIC SCHMIDT

First Toccata
(excerpt from Triptyque for Organ; Editions Henn-Chapuis)

ROGER VUATAZ

Flutes de joie
(excerpt from Diptyque de Concert; Op. 13; Editions Cantate Domino)

PIERRE SEGOND

Psalm 92
(Editions Scola Cantorum, Paris)

Francois Rabot, *Great Organ* of
St. Peter's Cathedral, Geneva

Timings:

Side 1: 11:08, 2:25, 2:25, 4:35, 2:42/23:35

Side 2: 3:33, 9:53, 1:34, 4:44, 3:42, 3:21/27:10

Musical Heritage Society

Musical Heritage Society Building
14 Park Road
Tinton Falls, New Jersey 07724

A "Genevan Organ School" was established at the end of th nineteenth century and has since acquired almost universa reknown. Its founder, Otto Barblan (1860-1943) studied with Immanuel Faisst in ... ...pointed organist fo Geneva's St ... the 55 year during ... ...organ and comp ... ...ducto of ...

MUSICAL HERITAGE SOCIETY
GENEVAN ORGAN MUSIC

MHS 3873
Side 1

STEREO
33 1/3 RPM

OTTO BARBLAN
Passacaille, Op. 6
ALEXANDRE MOTTU
Pour un jour de Contrition
Pour la fete de Paques
BERNARD REICHEL
Prelude grave
Prelude in E Minor

Francois RABOT,
Great Organ of St. Peter's Cathedral Geneva
Recorded by Phonotec
Licensed by Groupe Genevois
des Amis de L'Orgue

MUSICAL HERITAGE SOCIETY
GENEVAN ORGAN MUSIC

MHS 3873
Side 2

STEREO
33 1/3 RPM

HENRI GAGNEBIN
Psalm 150 - Bourdons, musettes
Dialogue et Pasacaille
Psalm XXIII
ERIC SCHMIDT
First Toccata
ROGER VUATAZ Flutes de joie
PIERRE SEGOND Psalm 92

Francois RABOT,
Great Organ of St. Peter's Cathedral Geneva
Recorded by Phonotec
Licensed by Groupe Genevois
des Amis de L'Orgue

(verso container)

Rabot, Francois.
    Genevan organ music [sound recording]. -- Tinton Falls,
N.J. : Musical Heritage Society, [1978].
    1 sound disc (51 min.) : analog, 33 1/3 rpm, stereo. ;
12 in.

    Musical Heritage Society: MHS 3873.
    Francois Rabot, playing the great organ of St. Peter's
Cathedral, Geneva.
    Editions recorded: Edition Peters no. 576; Editions
Salabert; Editions Cantate Domino Monthey; Editions Henn-
Chapuis; ms.; Editions Henn-Chapuis; Editions Cantate
Domino; Editions Schola Cantorum.
    Contents: Passac[a]ille, op. 6 / Otto Barblan (11:08)
-- Pour un jour de contrition ; Pour la fête de Paques /
Alexandre Mottu (2:25 ; 2:25) -- Prelude grave ; Prelude in
E minor / Bernard Reichel (4:35 ; 2:42) -- Psalm 150 ;
Dialogues et pa[s]sacaille ; Psalm XXIII / Henri Gagnebin
(3:33 ; 9:53 ; 1:34) -- First toccata / Eric Schmidt
(4:44) -- Flûtes de joie / Roger Vuataz (3:42) -- Psalm 92
/ Pierre Segond (3:21).

    I. Barblan, Otto, 1860-1943. Passacaglia, organ, op.
6, F minor. II. Mottu, Alexandre. Pieces liturques. Pour
un jour de contrition. III. Mottu, Alexandre. Pièces
liturgiques. Pour la fête de Paques. IV. Reichel, Bernard,
1901- Pièces, organ. Prelude grave. V. Reichel,
Bernard, 1901- Prelude, E minor. VI. Gagnebin, Henri, 1886-
Psalm 150. VII. Gagnebin, Henri, 1886- Dialogue et
passacaille, organ. VIII. Gagnebin, Henri, 1886- Psalm
XXIII. IX. Schmidt, Eric, 1907- Triptyque. Toccata,
no. 1. X. Vuataz, Roger, 1898- Diptyque de concert.
Flûtes de joie. XI. Segond, Pierre, 1913- Psalm 92.
XII. Title.

Again, this is a recording that would not be analyzed according to the current Library of Congress Rule
Interpretation for 21.7B. However, many academic libraries would provide the analysis without which these works
would probably not be retrievable. Some of the uniform titles (the Schmidt work for example) are based entirely on
the data that appear on this recording, because no other information is available in reference sources.

About The Artist

A strong love of simplicity and genuine home-made music
has led me to listen to, absorb and interpret songs and ballads
of thousands of anonymous singers from olden times. This love
for down-home music took hold when I was about nine or ten years
old in Charlotte, North Carolina and has continued to the present

I began my music studies with a ukulele in the late for
and "graduated" to the guitar soon after. My job as an edit
for the U.S. Department of Commerce took me to Washington,
in the sixties where I was first exposed to the five-stri
autoharp, mountain and hammered dulcimers. Ultimately I
a set of hand-made instrumernts which I use today virt
exclusion of those made in factories. These include:

Fretless Banjo, made by Donald Wilcox of Ann
Michigan in 1971.
Mountain dulcimers, one made by Dr. A.W. Jeff
Staunton, Virginia and the other by Kate Luke
Seaford, Virginia.
Hammered dulcimer and autoharp, both made by
Auterine of Montgomery, New York.

The lone non-handmade instrument I play is a c
style guitar made by the Yamaha folks of Japan.

These instruments, plus an abundant number of fi
and new songs, have taken me across North Carolina many
as well as numerous trips across the borders. Thanks to b
selected to participate in the North Carolina Visiting Arti
program in 1975, I have been able to share the instruments an
songs with city and country folk alike.

Side One

RHODODEND

the
mount   sp
wil
A

(5 p.; inserted in container)

FOLKWAYS Records
AND SERVICE CORP., 43 W. 61st ST., N.Y.C. 10023
Long Playing Non-Breakable Micro Groove 33⅓ RPM

EARLY AMERICAN FOLK
MUSIC AND SONGS
by CLARK JONES
Produced by JOHN R. CRAIG

SIDE 1   FTS 31091 A
                         Stereo

1. Rhododendron 2:16
2. The Rich Lady Over The Sea 2:30
3. I Will Give My Love An Apple 4:05
4. Under The Magnolia 1:51
5. The Holly Bears A Berry 3:44
6. Rye Whiskey 2:53
7. John Barleycorn 2:54
8. The Paw-Paw Patch :30
℗ © 1982 Folkways Records and Service Corp.

FOLKWAYS Records
AND SERVICE CORP., 43 W. 61st ST., N.Y.C. 10023
Long Playing Non-Breakable Micro Groove 33⅓ RPM

EARLY AMERICAN FOLK
MUSIC AND SONGS
by CLARK JONES
Produced by JOHN R. CRAIG

SIDE 2   FTS 31091 B
                         Stereo

1. Watermelon Suite 2:08
2. Beans, Bacon And Gravy 2:15
3. The Seeds Of Love 4.02
4. Aiken Drum 3:16
5. The Cherry Tree Carol 4:08
6. Young Man Who Wouldn't Hoe Corn 1:30
7. The Praties They Grow Small 2:05
8. Simple Gifts 1:23
℗ © 1982 Folkways Records and Service Corp.

(on verso container)

ABOUT THE ALB

Some of the songs on   gh while others
will evoke bittersweet memories.   make you want to do an
allemande left and a do-si-do and be child-like again, if only for a few
moments. The hope is that upon hearing the tunes and words of the
different selections you will feel better than you did before playing
the record.

By taking a glance at the song titles you will see that each one
relates in some way to plants — domestic flowers, wildflowers,
rees, vegetables, farm products, or foods and beverages obtained
om plants. Together, the songs make up a program that Clark has
rformed for the North Carolina Botanical Garden at Chapel Hill
ce 1973. These songs have been sung and played for the many
ors to the Garden, for economic botany final exams at the Univer-
to graduate bioloby students at Mountain Lake, Virginia (the
ersity of Virginia's Biological Station), and for numerous garden
s, schools and historical societies.

he program of songs about plants began shortly after Dr. C.
hie Bell, director of the Garden, began taking guitar lessons from
k. Dr. Bell has a great liking for folk songs and Clark enjoys hiking
d identifying wildflowers so the crossover of mutual interests led
tmately to the material on this record album.

This album is a mixture of history, music and botany (the non-
technical brand), and gives us some idea of the many different roles
that plants have played in our culture and lives for generations.

Produced by JOHN R. CRAIG
Recorded at STAR RECORDING COMPANY,
  Millers Creek, North Carolina.
Recording and Mixing Engineer: MARSHALL CRAVEN
Mixing: JOHN R. CRAIG
Photography: ANN HAWTHORNE

℗ © 1982 FOLKWAYS RECORDS & SERVICE CORP.
43 W. 61st ST., N.Y.C., 10023 N.Y., U.S.A.

Jones, Clark.
    Early American folk music and songs [sound recording] /
[performed] by Clark Jones. -- N.Y.C. [i.e. New York City],
N.Y. : Folkways Records, p1982.
    1 sound disc (42 min.) : analog, 33 1/3 rpm, stereo. ; 12
in.

    Folkways Records: FTS 31091.
    Clark Jones, vocals, hammered dulcimer, banjo, mountain
dulcimer, and guitar.
    Program notes on container; biographical and descriptive
notes (5 p.) in container.
    Contents: Rhododendron (2:16) -- The rich lady over the sea
(2:30) -- I will give my love an apple (4:05) -- Under the
magnolia (1:51) -- The holly bears a berry (3:44) -- Rye
whiskey (2:53) -- John Barleycorn (2:54) -- The paw-paw
patch (:30) -- Watermelon suite (2:08) -- Beans, bacon, and
gravy (2:15) -- The seeds of love (4:02) -- Aiken drum
(3:16) -- The cherry tree carol (4:08) -- Young man who
wouldn't hoe corn (1:30) -- The praties they grow small
(2:05) -- Simple gifts (1:23).

    I. Title.

Jones receives main entry here as principal performer. Note the misuse of the word "by" in the statement of
responsibility transcribed from the chief source. This is traditional music; none of it is composed by Jones.

In 1907 his family, in order to escape the prevalent Cossack terrors, managed to remove to New York City where very soon young Leo was awarded a scholarship to the Institute of Musical Art (later to become the Juilliard School of Music. Here he studied with Bertha Fiering Tapper, a fine pianist and teacher, who was to become an important figure in the development of Ornstein's creative career. In 1911 he made his public performing debut and within a few years he became a world-renowned young virtuoso with appearances not only in the U.S. but in the key musical centers of Europe. In 1913, after a childhood of conventional composition, he wrote his first "modern" work, the "Dwarf Suite" ("Suite des Gnomes"), the work recorded in the present album, which has been re-named, as befits present usage, "G[...] lished in London in 1915. [...] milarly expressionistic [...] turist, a member of a ra[...] to art the industrial and [...] advanced technology and [...] cities grown out of the a[...]

ARTHUR GOLD and ROBERT FIZDALE are probably the most successful "duo-pianists" in the world. Their concert circuit spans two continents. They have appeared with virtually every major orchestra in Europe and the U.S., as well as in their ov[...] ries'. They have made a great number of recordings a[...] television appearances.

One of the reasons for the important critical prestig[...] Fizdale is their enthusiastic performance of new work[...] porary composers: Milhaud, Poulenc, Virgil Thomson[...] eff, Bowles, Rorem, Rieti, and Cage, i.a.

Arthur Gold, senior by one year, was born in Toronto[...] oth w[...] ting w[...] solo c[...] t ever[...]

The present recording of the Sonata for Two Pianos was written on commission from the famous two-piano team of Gold and Fizdale, and was recorded by that ensemble for Columbia Records (CBS), from which this Serenus Recorded Edition is newly re-recorded. Alexei Haieff wrote the piece in 1945 when he was awarded a residence at the Yaddo Colony

(from verso container)

SERENUS RECORDED EDITIONS
SRS 12098A

LEO ORNSTEIN:
GNOMES' SUITE (Suite des Gnomes) 22'30"

Gnomes at Dawn	4'40"
Dance of the Gnomes	2'50"
Funeral March of the Gnomes	6'20"
Serenade of the Gnomes	- - -
Gnomes at Work	- - -
Marche Grotesque	8'30"

DWIGHT PELTZER, Piano

SRS 12098B   ALEXEI HAIEFF:
SONATA FOR TWO PIANOS   16'15"
Arthur GOLD and Robert FIZDALE

GNOMES' SUITE of Leo Ornstein is copyright and published by Joshua Corporation (BMI)   SONATA FOR TWO PIANOS of Alexei Haieff is copyright and published by General Music Publishing Co., Inc. (ASCAP)

138

```
Ornstein, Leo, 1892-
   [Gnomes' suite]
   Gnomes' suite = Suite des gnomes / Leo Ornstein.  Sonata for
two pianos / Alexei Haieff [sound recording]. -- Hastings-on-
Hudson, N.Y. : Serenus Recorded Editions, [1982?]
   1 sound disc (39 min.) : analog, 33 1/3 rpm, stereo. ; 12
in.

   Serenus Recorded Editions: SRS 12098
   Dwight Pelzer, piano (1st work) ; Arthur Gold and Robert
Fizdale, duo pianists (2nd work).
   Editions recorded: Joshua Corp.; General Music.
   The 2nd work re-recorded from Columbia Records.
   Program notes on container.
   Durations: 22:30; 16:15.

   I. Pelzer, Dwight.  II. Gold, Arthur.  III. Fizdale, Robert.
IV. Haieff, Alexei.  Sonatas, pianos (2).  V. Title.  VI.
Title: Suite des gnomes.
```

This example illustrates an art music recording with works by more than one composer, performed by different performers, and with no collective title. Transcription is similar to, although less complex than, the Temprees example above.

According to rule 21.23D, main entry is under the heading for the first work, therefore under the heading for the Ornstein work. Added entries are provided for the performers and for the other work.

The uniform title for the Ornstein work is an example of a later, better known title; Ornstein's original title for this work was *Dwarf suite*.

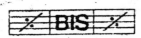

Recording Data: 1984-12-13/15 in the Petrus Church, Stocksund, Sweden
Recording Engineer & Digital Editing: Robert von Bahr
Sony PCM-F1 Digital Recording Equipment, 2 Schoeps CMC 541 U &
 2 Neumann U-89 Mics., SAM 82 Mixer, Sony Tape
Producer: Robert von Bahr
Cover Text: Lorentz Reitan
English Translation: John Skinner
German Translation: Per Skans
French Translation: Arlette Chené-Wiklander
Cover Photos: Hans Jorgen Brun, Bergen, Norway
Album Design: Robert von Bahr
Type-Setting: Marianne von Bahr
Lay-Out: William Jewson
Repro: KäPe Grafiska, Stockholm
Print: Offizin Paul Hartung, Hamburg, W. Germany 1985
CD-Production: Sanyo, Japan

© & ℗ : 1984 & 1985: Grammofon AB BIS

This record can be ordered from
Grammofon AB BIS
Väringavägen 6 S-182 63 Djursholm Sweden
Phone: Stockholm (08)/Int. + 168) - 755 41 00
Telex: 13880 bis s
or from BIS' agents all over the world   MADE IN WEST GER

(inside rear cover of booklet)

CD-291 STEREO
An original Digital recording

℗ & © : 1985,
Grammofon AB BIS

WIND QUINTETS
by Barber, Sæverud,
Jolivet & Hindemith
The BERGEN WIND QUINTET

BARBER, SAMUEL (1910-1981):
1. Summer Music for Woodwind Quintet Op. 31   (Schirmer)   11'26
SÆVERUD, HARALD (1897-   ):
Slåtter og stev fra „Siljustøl" Op. 21 a   (M/s)   13'00
  2. Kristi-blodsdråper (Fucsia) 1'32
  3. Dvergmålslått (Canzone dell'Ecó) 1'26
  4. Bå'nlåt (Ninnarella) 1'58
  5. Kvellingsull og Lokk (Vôce ed ombra nel vespero d'estate) 2'55
  6. Marcia Siljuana 4'53
JOLIVET, ANDRE (1905-1974)
Sérénade pour Quintette à vent
avec Hautbois principal (1945)   (Billaudot)   16'36
  7. Cantilene 4'18
  8. Caprice 3'14
  9. Intermède 4'
 10. Marche Burlesque 4'53
HINDEMITH, PAUL (1895-1963)
Kleine Kammermusik für fünf Bläser Op 24:2   13'40
 11. Lustig Mäßig schnelle Viertel 2'51
 12. Walzer. Durchweg sehr leise 2'06
 13. Ruhig und einfach 4'48
 14. Schnelle Viertel 1'49
 15. Sehr lebhaft 2'52

THE BERGEN WIND QUINTET

(verso container)

Bergen Blaserkvintett.
   Wind quintets [sound recording] / by Barber, Saeverud,
Jolivet & Hindemith. -- Djursholm, Sweden : Bis, p1985.
   1 sound disc (55 min.) : digital, stereo. ; 4 3/4 in.

   Bis: CD-291.
   The 2nd work originally for piano.
   Bergen Wind Quintet.
   Recorded Dec. 13-15, 1984, in the Petrus Church, Stocksund,
Sweden.
   Compact disc (indexed); digital recording.
   Notes in English, Swedish, German, and French ([12] p.) in
container.
   Also issued as analog disc: Bis LP-291.
   Contents: Summer music : for woodwind quintet, op. 31 /
Barber, Samuel (11:26) -- Slåtter og stev fra "Siljustøl" :
op. 21a / Saevurud, Harald (13:00) -- Sérénade pour
quintette à vent avec hautbois principal : 1945 / Jolivet,
André (16:36) -- Kleine Kammermusik : für funf Bläser, Op.
24:2 / Hindemith, Paul (13:40).

   I. Barber Samuel, 1910-   Summer music. II. Saeverud,
Harold, 1897-   Slåtter og stev fra Siljustøl, op. 21;
arr. III. Jolivet, André, 1905-1974. Sérénades, wind
quintet (1945). IV. Hindemith, Paul, 1895-1963. Kleine
Kammermusik.

This is a compact disc. Note the placement of the term "digital" in the other physical details area of the physical description, indicating the *playback* mechanism, and the physical description *note*, indicating the characteristics of the disc and the *recording* mechanism.

    Main entry is under the heading for the principal performer. Analytical added entries are required for each of the works. No title added entry is supplied because the title would be meaningless alone. (cf. MCD 21.30J).

ALBAN BERG
Lulu Suite
Lyric Suite

VOX CUM LAUDE
MCD 10024

© 1983 THE MOSS MUSIC GROUP, INC. • ALL RIGHTS RESERVED • UNAUTHORIZED DUPLICATION IS A VIOLATION OF APPLICABLE LAWS

Kathleen Battle, Soprano
Cincinnati Symphony Orchestra
Michael Gielen, Conductor

(verso booklet)

30024-2

COMPACT DISC
DIGITAL AUDIO

AN ORIGINAL DIGITAL RECORDING

ALBAN BERG

Kathleen Battle, Soprano
Cincinnati Symphony Orchestra
Michael Gielen, Conductor

Lulu Suite (34:33)
Rondo: Andante und Hymne (Tr. 1–15:37)
Ostinato: Allegro (Tr. 2–3:31)
Lied der Lulu: Comodo* (Tr. 3–2:33)
Variationen: Moderato (Tr. 4–3:34)
Adagio: Sostenuto; Lento; Grave* (Tr. 5–8:54)

*with Kathleen Battle, Soprano

Lyric Suite (16:06)
Andante amoroso (Tr. 6–6:00)
Allegro misterioso (Tr. 7–3:44)
Adagio appassionato (Tr. 8–6:10)

Vox Cum Laude
MMG
MCD 10024

(verso container)

```
Berg, Alban, 1885-1935.
   [Lulu.  Suite]
   Lulu suite ; Lyric suite [sound recording] / Alban Berg.
-- New York, N.Y. : Vox Cum Laude, p1983.
   1 sound disc (51 min.) : digital ; 4 3/4 in.

   Vox Cum Laude: MCD 10024.
   The 2nd work originally for string quartet.
   Kathleen Battle, soprano (1st work) ; Cincinnati Symphony
Orchestra ; Michael Gielen, conductor.
   Recorded Sept. 2-4, 1981.
   Compact disc (indexed); digital recording.
   Durations: 34:33 ; 16:06.
   Program notes, including German text of 1st work with
English translation (11 p.), in container.

   I: Battle, Kathleen.  II. Gielen, Michael, 1927-    III.
Berg, Alban, 1885-1935.  Lyrische Suite.  Selections; arr.
IV. Cincinnati Symphony Orchestra.  V. Title.  VI. Title:
Lyric suite.
```

This compact disc is described in much the same way as the preceding example. Note, however, that "stereo." does not appear in the physical description area, because the recording itself does not indicate that it is stereophonic.

Main entry is under the heading for Berg, who composed both works, with the uniform title for the first work. An analytical added entry is made for the second work, and added entries are made for the principal performers. Two title added entries are formulated to create unique access points for both titles included in area 1.

Enregistrement numérique/Digital recording/Digital-Aufnahme
Direction artistique de l'enregistrement/Recording supervision/Aufnahmeleitung :
Michel Garcin
Ingénieur du son/Sound engineer/Tonmeister : Yolanta Skura
Montage musical/Editing/Schnitt : Françoise Garcin
Enregistrement réalisé en/Recording/Aufnahme : juillet/July/Juli 1984,
Queen's Hall, Edinburgh

Disponible en/Available in/Auch erhältlich als :
● NUM 75183 & ·· MCE 75183

© Editions Costallat 1985

Photo Peter K. Elkus, New York - Maquette Daniel et C°
Imprimé en Allemagne Printed in West Germany

(verso booklet)

ECD 88100

FREDERICA
VON STADE
chante

Monteverdi
Cavalli

The Scottish
Chamber Orchestra

Direction :
Raymond LEPPARD

Enregistrement numérique

ERATO

℗ Editions Costallat 1985
Made in W.-Germany

3 269658 810028

ERATO

ERATO

ECD 88100

FREDERICA VON STADE CHANTE MONTEVERDI/CAVALLI - ECD 88100

FREDERICA VON STADE CHANTE MONTEVERDI/CAVALLI - ECD 88100

(verso container)

Claudio MONTEVERDI
(1567-1643)

1. OHIMÈ CH'IO CADO 5'34

2. LAMENTO DI OTTAVIA : 6'11
   "Disprezzata Regina"
   (L'Incoronazione di Poppea)

3. ET È PUR DUNQUE VERO 8'06
   (Scherzi Musicali, 1632)

4. ARIA DI OTTAVIA : 4'01
   "A Dio Roma..."
   (L'Incoronazione di Poppea)

Francesco CAVALLI
(1602-1676)

5. LAMENTO DI CASSANDRA : 5'0
   "L'alma fiacca svanì"
   (La Didone)

6. LA BELLEZZA E UN DON
   FUGACE 2'30
   (Xerce)

7. LAMENTO DI CLORI : 6'10
   "Amor, che ti die l'ali"
   (L'Egisto)

8. NUMI CIECHI PIÙ DI ME 3'10
   (L'Ormonte)

9. NON È, NON E CRUDEL 3'30
   (Scipione africano)

10. ARDO, SOSPIRO E PIANGO 3'32
    (Calisto)

FREDERICA VON STADE, mezzo soprano

THE SCOTTISH CHAMBER ORCHESTRA
RAYMOND LEPPARD

(Réalisation : Raymond Leppard, Faber Music, London)

℗ Editions Costallat 1985

Imprimé en Allemagne Printed in West Germany Made in West Germany

RC 650
QA

DDD

Von Stade, Frederica.
    Frederica von Stade chante Monteverdi, Cavalli [sound recording]. -- [France] : Erato, p1985.
    1 sound disc (48 min.) : digital ; 4 3/4 in.

    Erato: ECD 88100.
    Sung in Italian.
    Frederica von Stade, mezzo-soprano ; Scottish Chamber Orchestra ; Raymond Leppard, conductor.
    Recorded July 1984, Queen's Hall, Edinburgh.
    Program notes in French, English, and German ([8] p.) in container.
    Compact disc (indexed).
    Also issued as LP (Erato NUM 75183) and cassette (Erato MCE 75183).
    Contents: Ohimè ch'io cado (5:34) ; Lamento di Ottavia "Disprezzata Regina" (L'Incoronazione di Poppea) (6:11) ; Et è pur dunque vero (Scherzi musicali, 1632) (8:06) ; Aria di Ottavia "A Dio Roma" (L'Incoronazione di Poppea) (4:01) / Claudio Monteverdi -- Lamento di Cassandra "L'alma fiacca svani" (La Didone) (5:02) ; La Belleza è un Don Fugace (Xerce) (2:30) ; Lamento di Clori "Amor, che ti die l'ali" (L'Edisto) (6:10) ; Numi Ciechi più di me (L'Orimonte) (3:10) ; Non è, Non è crudel (Scipione africano) (3:30) ; Ardo, sospiro e piango (Calisto) (3:32).

    I. Leppard, Raymond. II. Scottish Chamber Orchestra. III. Title.

This compact disc, like many others, was released simultaneously with analog LP and cassette versions. Otherwise, with the exception of the physical description, this cataloging is identical to cataloging for an LP. Note that the *label-name* is recorded in place of the publisher's name in area 4.

Main entry is under the heading for Von Stade as principal performer. Because this falls into the category of "recital" recordings (cf. RI 21.7B) no analytical added entries are made for the works performed. Added entries are made for the other performers.

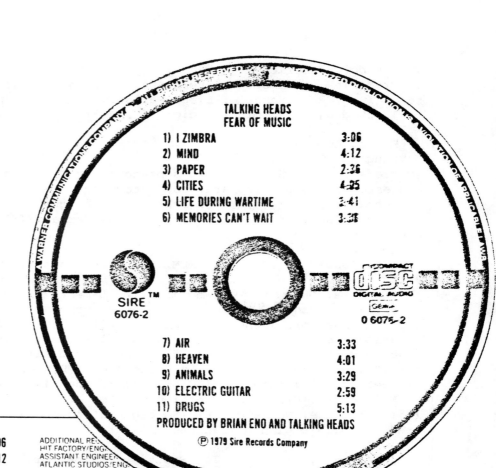

(booklet, p. 1)

1) I ZIMBRA   3:06
2) MIND   4:12
3) PAPER   2:36
4) CITIES   4:05
5) LIFE DURING WARTIME   3:41
6) MEMORIES CAN'T WAIT   3:30
7) AIR   3:33
8) HEAVEN   4:01
9) ANIMALS   3:29
10) ELECTRIC GUITAR   2:59
11) DRUGS   5:13

PRODUCED BY BRIAN ENO AND TALKING HEADS

BAND MEMBERS:

DAVID BYRNE
JERRY HARRISON
TINA WEYMOUTH
CHRIS FRANTZ

BRIAN ENO: TREATMENTS

GENE WILDER AND ARI: CONGAS ON "LIFE DURING
WARTIME" AND "I ZIMBRA"
ROBERT FRIPP: GUITAR ON "I ZIMBRA"
(APPEARS COURTESY OF E.G. RECORDS LTD.)
THE SWEETBREATHES: BACKGROUND VOCALS ON "AIR"
JULIE LAST, BRIAN ENO, DAVID BYRNE: BACKGROUND
VOCALS ON "I ZIMBRA"
THE BIRDS ON "DRUGS" RECORDED AT LONE PINE
KOALA SANCTUARY, BRISBANE, AUSTRALIA

ALL BASIC TRACKS RECORDED AT CHRIS AND TINA'S
LOFT IN LONG ISLAND CITY, WITH THE RECORD PLANT
REMOTE TRUCK ON APRIL 22 AND MAY 6, 1979
ENGINEER: ROD O'BRIAN
CREW: DAVE HEWITT, FRED RIDDER, PHIL GITOMER,
YOSTER McALLISTER

ADDITIONAL RE...
HIT FACTORY/ENG...
ASSISTANT ENGINEER...
ATLANTIC STUDIOS/ENG...
ASSISTANT ENGINEER: TIM...
RPM SOUND STUDIOS/ENGINEER...
RECORD PLANT/ENGINEER: ROD O'B...
LP ORIGINALLY MASTERED AT STERLING SOUN...
CALBI.
CDD PRE-MASTERING BY WCI RECORD GROUP

LIVE SOUND: FRANK GALLAGHER
ROAD COORDINATION: ACE PENNA

COVER CONCEPT: JERRY HARRISON
THERMOGRAPH (HEAT SENSITIVE PHOTO)
BY JIMMY GARCIA COURTESY DR. PHILLIP STRAX
© 1979 SIRE RECORDS COMPANY
CONCEPT: DAVID WITH JERRY'S HELP

MANAGEMENT: GARY KURFIRST, OVERLAND
PRODUCTIONS, 1775 BROADWAY, 7TH FLOOR,
NEW YORK, NY 10019

ALL SONGS WRITTEN BY DAVID BYRNE EXCEPT "I
ZIMBRA" WRITTEN BY D. BYRNE/B. ENO/H. BALL
ALL SONGS © 1979 INDEX MUSIC/BLEU DISQUE MUSIC
CO., INC. ASCAP EXCEPT "I ZIMBRA" PUBLISHED BY
INDEX MUSIC/BLEU DISQUE MUSIC CO., INC. ASCAP/E.G
MUSIC, LTD. BMI. ALL RIGHTS RESERVED.

...GALLASSA...

A BIM BERI GLASS...
E GLASSALA TUFF...

GADJI BERI BIMBA...
LAULI LONNI CADO...
A BIM BERI GLASS...
E GLASSALA TUFF...

MIND

TIME WON'T CHANG...
MONEY WON'T CHA...
I HAVEN'T GOT THE...
EVERYTHING SEEM...

I NEED SOMETHING...

DRUGS WON'T CHA...
RELIGION WON'T C...

SCIENCE WON'T C...
LOOKS LIKE I CAN'T...
I TRY TO TALK TO Y...
BUT YOU'RE NOT E...
AND IT COMES DIR...

I NEED SOMETHING...

PAPER

HOLD THE PAPER...
(SOME DAYS PASS...
EXPOSE YOURSEL...
(SOME DAYS PASS...

TAKE A LITTLE RE...
TAKE A LITTLE TIM...
THROUGH...

```
Byrne, David, 1952-
     Fear of music [sound recording] / Talking Heads. -- [New
York] : Sire Records, p1979.
     1 sound disc (41 min.) : digital ; 4 3/4 in.

     Sire Records: 6076-2.
     Rock music.
     "All songs written by David Byrne except 'I Zimbra' written
by D. Byrne, B. Eno, H. Ball."
     Recorded in Long Island City, N.Y., April 22 and May 6,
1979.
     Song texts ([8] p.) in container.
     Compact disc; analog recording.
     Contents: I Zimbra (3:06) -- Mind (4:12) -- Paper (2:36)
-- Cities (4:05) -- Life during wartime (3:41) -- Memories
can't wait (3:30) -- Air (3:33) -- Heaven (4:01) -- Animals
(3:29) -- Electric guitar (2:59) -- Drugs (5:13).

     I. Talking Heads (Musical group).  II. Title.
```

An early compact disc, this rock music recording was remastered from an analog tape, which is duly noted. The main entry is under the heading for David Byrne, who composed all the music. Most rock recordings would be entered under the heading for the principal performer because they are considered to be anthologies. Note, however, that this information is buried in the accompanying booklet.

(container)

Brahms, Johannes, 1833-1897.
    [Symphonies, no. 4, op. 98, E minor]
    Symphony no. 4 in E minor, op. 98 [sound recording] /
Brahms. -- [Minneapolis, Minn.] : Quintessence, [197-?]
    1 sound cassette : 1 7/8 ips, stereo., Dolby processed.
-- (Critic's choice)

    Quintessence: P4C-7094.
    Title from container.
    Czech Philharmonic Orchestra ; Dietrich Fischer-Dieskau,
conductor.

    I. Fischer-Dieskau, Dietrich, 1925-   II. Cesk'a
filharmonie. III. Series.

This is a typical cassette recording. Note that there is no title information on the cassette itself.

149

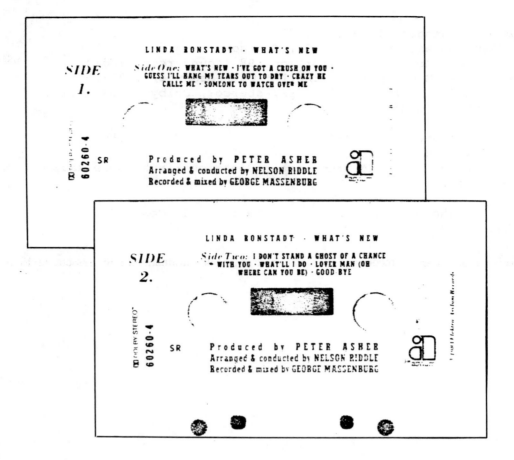

LINDA RONSTADT · WHAT'S NEW

SIDE 1.

Side One: WHAT'S NEW · I'VE GOT A CRUSH ON YOU · GUESS I'LL HANG MY TEARS OUT TO DRY · CRAZY HE CALLS ME · SOMEONE TO WATCH OVER ME

60260-4   SR

Produced by PETER ASHER
Arranged & conducted by NELSON RIDDLE
Recorded & mixed by GEORGE MASSENBURG

LINDA RONSTADT · WHAT'S NEW

SIDE 2.

Side Two: I DON'T STAND A GHOST OF A CHANCE WITH YOU · WHAT'LL I DO · LOVER MAN (OH WHERE CAN YOU BE) · GOOD-BYE

60260-4   SR

Produced by PETER ASHER
Arranged & conducted by NELSON RIDDLE
Recorded & mixed by GEORGE MASSENBURG

(verso container insert)

(℗ 1983)

WHAT'S NEW

ARRANGED & CONDUCTED BY NELSON RIDDLE

PRODUCED BY PETER ASHER

RECORDED & MIXED BY GEORGE MASSENBURG

Assisted by Barbara Rooney & Robert Spano

Recorded at The Complex (L.A.) June 30th, 1982 — March 4th, 1983

Mastered by Doug Sax at the Mastering Lab (L.A.)

Photography by Brian Aris

Art direction and design by Kosh with Ron Larson

Album coordination by Gloria Boyce

Special thanks to George for his help with the vocals, and to

John Neal for his advice during the recording.

Piano: Don Grolnick

Guitar: Tommy Tedesco or Dennis Budimir

Bass: Ray Brown or James Hughart

Drums: John Guerin

Concertmasters: Leonard Atkins & Nathan Ross

Ronstadt, Linda.
    What's new [sound recording] / Linda Ronstadt ; arranged & conducted by Nelson Riddle. -- [New York, N.Y.] : Asylum, p1983.
    1 sound cassette : 1 7/8 ips, stereo., Dolby processed.

    Asylum: 60260-4.
    Linda Ronstadt, vocals ; Nelson Riddle Orchestra ; Nelson Riddle, conductor.
    Recorded at the Complex, Los Angeles, June 30th, 1982-Mar. 4th, 1983.
    Contents: What's new -- I've got a crush on you -- Guess I'll hang my tears out to dry -- Crazy he calls me -- Someone to watch over me -- I don't stand a ghost of a chance with you -- What I'll do -- Lover man (oh where can you be) -- Good bye.

    I. Riddle, Nelson. II. Nelson Riddle Orchestra. III. Title.

A cassette issue of this popular music recording. Note that Riddle's name is transcribed in the statement of responsibility because he is given credit for the arrangements (orchestrations) of these songs. The physical description is limited because this is a standard cassette.

Main entry is under the heading for Ronstadt, the principal performer. Riddle and his orchestra receive added entries.

CHAPTER 6: A MUSIC CATALOGER'S REFERENCE COLLECTION

CATALOGING

These publications are of major importance to music catalogers because they announce policy and interpretations from the Library of Congress.

Cataloging Service Bulletin. Washington, D.C.: Library of Congress, 1978-

> Available from: Cataloging Distribution Service, Library of Congress, Washington, D.C., 20541.

Music Cataloging Bulletin. Canton, Mass.: Music Library Association, 1970-

> Available from: Music Library Association, P.O. Box 487, Canton, MA 02021.

---. *Supplement to Volume 1-5, 1970-1974.* Comp. and ed. by Ruth Henderson. Ann Arbor, Mich.: Music Library Association, 1976.

---. *Index/Supplement to Volumes 6-10, 1975-1979.* Comp. and ed. by Marguerite Iskenderian. Philadelphia: Music Library Association, 1980.

---. *Index/Supplement to Volumes 11-15, 1980-1984.* Comp. and ed. by Marguerite Iskenderian. Canton, Mass.: Music Library Association, 1985.

> The three supplements include cumulations of changes in classification, subject headings, and personal, corporate, and uniform title headings; also included is a cumulation of the column "New Reference Books in the Music Section." Available from the Music Library Association, as above.

GENERAL MUSIC REFERENCE

Apel, Willi. *Harvard Dictionary of Music.* 2nd ed. Cambridge: Belknap Press, 1969.

> Excellent source for definition of musical terms.

Duckles, Vincent. *Music Reference and Research Materials: An Annotated Bibliography.* 3rd ed. New York: Free Press, 1974.

> General guide to major music reference tools, this is the "Mudge" (Winchell/Sheehy) of music librarianship.

Heyer, Anna Harriet. *Historical Sets, Collected Editions, and Monuments of Music: A Guide to their Contents.* 3rd ed. Chicago: American Library Association, 1980.

> Fast way to locate complete works of composers; useful for locating composers' original titles when no thematic index is available.

Krummel, Donald W. *Guide for Dating Early Published Music: a Manual of Bibliographical Practices.* Hackensack, N.J.: J. Boonin, 1974.

Marco, Guy A. *Information on Music: A Handbook of Reference Sources in European Languages.* Littleton, Colo.: Libraries Unlimited, 1975-

---. Volume 1: *Basic and universal sources.* With the assistance of Sharon Paugh Ferris.

> Less convenient to use but more up-to-date than Duckles.

Thorin, Suzanne E., and Carole Franklin Vidali. *The Acquisition and Cataloging of Music and Sound Recordings: A Glossary.* MLA Technical Report no. 11. Canton, Mass.: Music Library Association, 1984.

> Although this pamphlet suffers from some editorial problems, it is a comprehensive glossary of terms encountered frequently by music librarians.

ACCESS TO SOUND RECORDINGS

Billboard ... International Buyer's Guide. New York: Billboard Publications, 1963-

Useful for determining which labels are owned by which companies, etc. Reissued (updated) biennially.

Phonolog Reports. Los Angeles: Phonolog Publishing Division, 1948-

Useful for identifying record labels, manufacturers, distributors, etc. Also handy for determining the origin of printed folios (i.e., those that are printed transcriptions of sound recordings). Also useful for authority work for current recording artists. Usually available for consultation in record stores.

Schwann-1 Record and Tape Guide. Boston: Schwann Record Catalogs, 1949-

Monthly guide to currently available sound recordings in the U.S.; includes monthly lists of new releases.

BIOBIBLIOGRAPHY

ENGLISH LANGUAGE

Anderson, E. Ruth. *Contemporary American Composers: A Biographical Dictionary.* 2nd ed. Boston: G.K. Hall, 1982.

Baker's Biographical Dictionary of Musicians. 7th ed. Rev. by Nicolas Slonimsky. New York: Schirmer Books; London: Collier Macmillan, c1984.

The International Cyclopedia of Music and Musicians. 11th ed. Edited by Bruce Bohle. New York: Dodd, Mead, 1985.

The New Grove Dictionary of Music and Musicians. 20 vols. Edited by Stanley Sadie. London: Macmillan; Washington: Grove's Dictionaries, 1980.

Southern, Eileen. *Biographical Dictionary of Afro-American and African Musicians.* Westport, Conn.: Greenwood Press, 1982.

Vinton, John. *Dictionary of Contemporary Music.* New York: E. P. Dutton, 1974.

FRENCH LANGUAGE

Encyclopédie de la musique. 3 vols. Paris: Fasquelle, [1958-1961].

Honegger, Marc. *Dictionnaire de la musique.* 3 vols. N.p.: Bordas, 1970.

Larousse de la musique. 2 vols. Publié sous la direction de Norbert Dufourcq. Paris: Larousse, 1957.

GERMAN LANGUAGE

Brockhaus Riemann Musiklexikon. 2 vols. Herausgegeben von Carl Dahlhaus und Hans Heinrich Eggebrecht. Wiesbaden: Brockhaus, 1978.

Die Musik in Geschichte und Gegenwart. 14 vols. Edited by Friedrich Blume. Kassel u. Basel: Bärenreiter, 1949-1967.

Riemann, Hugo. *Musik-Lexikon.* 5 vols. Mainz: B. Schott's Söhne, 1959-1972.

ITALIAN LANGUAGE

Dizionario Ricordi della musica e dei musicisti. Dirretore: Claudio Sartori; redattori, Fausto Broussard et al. Milano: Ricordi, 1959.

POPULAR MUSIC

Claghorn, Charles Eugene. *Biographical Dictionary of Jazz.* Englewood Cliffs, N. J.: Prentice-Hall, 1982.

The Rolling Stone Encyclopedia of Rock & Roll. Edited by Jon Pareles and Patty Romanowski. 1st ed. New York: Rolling Stone Press/Summit Books, 1983.

Stambler, Erwin. *Encyclopedia of Folk, Country, and Western Music.* Rev. ed., 1st ed. New York: St. Martin's Press, 1982.

The Year in Rock ... From the editors of *Musician: Player & Listener.* New York: Delilah Books, 1981.

THEMATIC INDEXES

Brook, Barry S. *Thematic Catalogues in Music: An Annotated Bibliography* ... Hillsdale, N.Y.: Pendragon Press, 1972.

Good source for finding thematic catalogs for most major composers. Should be used in conjunction with the following list of approved thematic indexes, issued for the Library of Congress in *Music Cataloging Bulletin*, arranged here in alphabetical order by composer indexed. For instructions on the use of thematic index numbers in uniform titles see Chapter 5.

ALBINONI, TOMASO, 1671-1750.

   Giazotto, Remo. *Tomaso Albinoni: Musico di violino dilettante veneto.* Milan, Bocca, 1945.

BACH, CARL PHILIPP EMANUEL, 1714-1788.

   Wotquenne, Alfred. *Thematisches Verzeichnis der Werke von C.P.E. Bach.* Wiesbaden: Breitkopf & Härtel, 1964.

BACH, JOHANN CHRISTOPH FRIEDRICH, 1732-1795.

   Wohlfarth, Hannsdieter. *Johann Christoph Friedrich Bach: Ein Komponist im Vorfeld der Klassik.* Bern: Francke Verlag, 1971.

BACH, JOHANN SEBASTIAN, 1685-1750.

   Schmieder, Wolfgang. *Thematisch-systematisches Verzeichnis der Musikalischen Werke von Johann Sebastian Bach, Bach-Werke Verzeichnis (BWV).* Leipzig: Breitkopf & Härtel, 1950.

BACH, WILHELM FRIEDEMAN, 1710-1784.

   Falck, Martin. *Wilhelm Friedemann Bach: Sein Leben und seine Werke mit thematischem Verzeichnis seiner Kompositionen.* Leipzig: Kahnt, 1919.

BEETHOVEN, LUDWIG VAN, 1770-1827.

   Kinsky, Georg and Hans Halm. *Das Werk Beethovens: Thematisch-bibliographisches Verzeichnis seiner sämtlichen vollendeten Kompositionen.* München: G. Henle, 1955.

BENDA, FRANZ, 1709-1786.

   Lee, Douglas A. *Franz Benda, 1709-1786: A Thematic Catalogue of his Works.* New York: Pendragon Press, 1984.

BOCCHERINI, LUIGI, 1745-1805.

   Gerard, Yves. *Catalogue of the Works of Luigi Boccherini.* London: Oxford University Press, 1969.

BULL, JOHN, d. 1628.

   Steele, John, Francis Camerin, and Thurston Dart, eds. *John Bull: Keyboard Music.* 2 vols. Musica Britannica, vols. 14 and 19. London: Stainer and Bell, 1960-1963.

BUXTEHUDE, DIETRICH, 1637-1707.

   Karstadt, Georg. *Thematisch-systematisch Verzeichnis der musikalischen Werke von Dietrich Buxtehude.* Wiesbaden: Breitkopf & Härtel, 1974.

CHARPENTIER, MARC ANTOINE, 1634-1704.

   Hitchcock, H. Wiley. "Charpentier, Marc-Antoine." In *The New Grove Dictionary of Music and Musicians,* 4:162-176. London: Macmillan; Washington: Grove's Dictionaries, 1980.

   ---. *Les oeuvres de Marc-Antoine Charpentier: Catalogue raisonné.* Paris: Picard, 1982.

CLEMENTI, MUZIO, 1752-1832.

> Tyson, Alan. *Thematic Catalogue of the Works of Muzio Clementi*. Tutzing: Hans Schneider, 1967.

COPERARIO, JOHN, 1570 (ca.)-1626.

> Charteris, Richard. *John Coprario: A Thematic Catalogue of his Music*. New York: Pendragon Press, 1977.

EYBLER, JOSEPH, EDLER VON, 1765-1846.

> Herrmann, Hildegard. *Thematisches Verzeichnis der Werke von Joseph Eybler*. München: E. Katzbichler, 1976.

FREDERICK II, KING OF PRUSSIA, 1712-1786.

> "Thematisches Verzeichniss der Flötensonaten." In *Musikalische Werke Friedrichs des Grossen*, vol. 1. Leipzig: Breitkopf & Härtel, 1889.

GABRIELI, GIOVANNI, 1557-1612.

> Kenton, Egon. *Life and Works of Giovanni Gabrieli*. N.p.: American Institute of Musicology, 1967.

GARCIA, JOSE MAURICIO NUNES, 1767-1830.

> Mattos, Cleofe Person de. *Catalogo tematico das obras do Padre José Mauricio Nunes García*. Rio de Janeiro: Ministerio da Educacao e Cultura, 1970.

GASSMANN, FLORIAN LEOPOLD, 1729-1774.

> Hill, George R. *A Thematic Catalog of the Instrumental Music of Florian Leopold Gassmann*. Hackensack, N.J.: J. Boonin, 1976.

GRIFFES, CHARLES TOMLINSON, 1884-1920.

> Anderson, Donna K. *The Works of Charles T. Griffes: A Descriptive Catalogue*. Ann Arbor: UMI Research Press, 1983.

HANDEL, GEORG FRIDERIC, 1685-1759.

> Bell, A. Craig. *Handel: Chronological Thematic Catalogue*. Darley: Grian-Aig Press, 1972.

HAYDN, JOSEPH, 1732-1809.

> Hoboken, Anthony van. *Joseph Haydn: Thematisch-bibliographisches Werkverzeichnis*. 2 vols. Mainz: B. Schott's Söhne, 1957-1971.

HOFFMEISTER, FRANZ ANTON, 1754-1812.

> Hoffmeister, Franz Anton. *Two symphonies, them. index D1, G5*. Edited by Roger Hickman. The Symphony, 1720-1840, ser. B, v. 5. New York: Garland, 1984.

MOZART, WOLFGANG AMADEUS, 1756-1791.

> Kochel, Ludwig Ritter von. *Chronologisch-thematisches Verzeichniss* [sic] *sämmtlicher Tonwerke W. A. Mozarts*. 6 Aufl. Wiesbaden: Breitkopf & Härtel, 1964.

NOVOTNY, FERENC, ca. 1749-1806.

> Novotny, Ferenc. *The Symphony in Hungary: Thematic Index 1, 2.* Edited by Dorottya Somorjay. The symphony, 1720-1840, ser. B, v. 12. New York: Garland, 1984.

PLEYEL, IGNAZ, 1757-1831.

> Benton, Rita. *Ignace Pleyel: A Thematic Catalogue of his Compositions.* New York: Pendragon Press, 1977.

PURCELL, HENRY, 1659-1795.

> Zimmerman, Franklin B. *Henry Purcell, 1659-1695: An Analytical Catalogue of his Music.* London: Macmillan, 1963.

QUANTZ, JOHANN JOACHIM, 1697-1773.

> Kohler, Karl-Heinz. "Die Triosonate bei den Dresdener Zeitgenossen J.S. Bachs." Dissertation. Jena, 1956.

> Numbers may be deduced from: Reilly, Edward R. *Quantz and his "Versuch": Three Studies.* New York: American Musicological Society, 1971.

RYBA, JAKUB JAN, 1765-1815.

> Němecek, Jan. *Jakub Jan Ryba: Zivot a dilo.* Praha: Státní Hudební Vydavatelství, 1963.

SCARLATTI, DOMENICO, 1685-1757.

> Kirkpatrick, Ralph. *Domenico Scarlatti.* 6th corrected printing. Princeton, N.J.: Princeton University Press, 1970.

> Scarlatti, Domenico. *Complete Keyboard Works in Facsimile from the Manuscript and Printed Sources.* 18 vols. Edited by Ralph Kirkpatrick. New York: Johnson Reprint Corp., 1972.

SCHUBERT, FRANZ, 1797-1828.

> Deutsch, Otto Erich. *Schubert: Thematic Catalogue of all his works in Chronological Order.* London: Dent, 1951.

SOLER, ANTONIO, 1729-1783.

> Soler, Antonio. *Sonatas for Piano.* Edited by Frederick Marvin. New York: Continuo Music Press, 1976.

STRAUSS, RICHARD, 1864-1949.

> Mueller von Asow, E. H. *Richard Strauss: Thematisches Verzeichnis.* 3 vols. Wien: L. Doblinger, 1959-1974.

TARTINI, GIUSEPPE, 1692-1770.

> Dounias, Minos. *Die Violinkonzerte G. Tartinis als Ausdruck einer Kunstlerpersönlichkeit und einer Kulturrepoche: Mit vielen Notenbeispielen und einem thematischen Verzeichnis.* Wolfenbüttel: Kallmeyer, 1935. Reprint. Wolfenbüttel: Möseler, 1966.

TORELLI, GIUSEPPE, 1658-1709.

    Giegling, Franz. *Giuseppe Torelli: Ein Beitrag zur Entwicklungsgeschichte des italienischen Konzerts.* Kassel: Bärenreiter, 1949.

VIOTTI, GIOVANNI BATTISTA, 1755-1824.

    White, Chappel. *Giovanni Battista Viotti, 1755-1824: A Thematic Catalogue of his Works.* New York: Pendragon Press, 1985.

VIVALDI, ANTONIO, 1678-1741.

    Ryom, Peter. *Verzeichnis der Werke Antonio Vivaldis.* Kleine Ausg. Leipzig: Deutsche Verlag für Musik, 1974.

    --- . *Antonio Vivaldi: table de concordances des oeuvres (RV).* Kobenhavn: Engstrom & Sodring, 1973.

        Indispensable for translating numbers from the Pincherle and Fanna catalogs (used with earlier rules) into Ryom numbers.

VOGLER, GEORG JOSEPH, 1749-1814.

    Schaufhautl, Karl Emil von. *Abt Georg Joseph Vogler.* Ausburg: M. Huttler, 1888. Reprint. Hildesheim: Georg Olms, 1979.

WAGENSEIL, GEORG CHRISTOPH, 1715-1777.

    Scholz-Michelitsch, Helga. *Das Klavierwerk von Georg Christoph Wagenseil: Thematischer Katalog.* Tabulae musicae Austricae, Bd. 3. Wien: Bohlau, 1966.

    ---. *Das Orchester- und Kammermusik von Georg Christoph Wagenseil: Thematischer Katalog.* Tabulae musicae Austricae, Bd. 6. Wien: Bohlau, 1972.

WEISS, SILVIUS LEOPOLD, 1686-1750.

    Klima, Josef. *Silvius Leopold Weiss: Kompositionen für die Laute, Quellen- und Themenverzeichnis.* Wien: J. Klima, 1975.

GLOSSARY

This glossary contains definitions of terms that are peculiar to music cataloging or to this text. Terms already defined in *AACR 2* are not included here, unless the usage in this manual differs from the definition given in *AACR 2*. Terms frequently encountered in the practice of music librarianship are defined in *The Acquisition and Cataloging of Music and Sound Recordings*. Definitions of musical terms can be found in the *Harvard Dictionary of Music* and *The New Grove's Dictionary*. (For complete bibliographical information on these sources, see Chapter 6.)

Accompanying material. (1) For *printed music*, introductory prose, often biographical or editorial in nature, appearing on pages preceding or (less often) following the music itself. (2) Occasionally, in twentieth century music, a tape recording intended to be used in performance or realization of the composition. (3) For *sound recordings*, prose (often referred to as "program notes"), printed on the container, usually biographical or historical. Occasionally, a separate pamphlet containing such prose, with or without a libretto or score of the musical work.

Collective title. An inclusive title proper for a sound recording containing recordings of more than one musical work. A collective title may appear on the label(s), the **container**, or in the **accompanying material**.

Container (Sound recording). A protective slipcase or box (as opposed to a **sleeve**) that holds one or more sound recordings, and from which the recordings must be removed to be played.

Cover. For printed music, a folder whether attached or detached, wrapped around the printed music, and made of substantially different material (heavier or different colored paper) than the paper on which the music is printed. See also **Decorative title page**.

Decorative title page. A title page for printed music, made of the same material as the paper on which the music is printed, and bearing a substantial illustration (often in lieu of a **cover**). See also **Cover**.

Distinctive title. (1) A title proper for musical work that does not consist of the name of a type of composition, or of one or more names of types of composition and a connector ("and," etc.), (e.g., *Lincoln Portrait*). (2) A title proper for a musical work that consists of the name of a type of composition modified by an adjective (e.g., *Little suite*). See also **Generic title**; **Type of composition**.

Duration. The playing time of a musical work.

Excerpts. Separately published and/or recorded segments of a musical work.

Generic title. A title proper for a musical work that consists of the name(s) of one or more types of composition (e.g., fugue, sonata, divertimento, piece, etc.). See also **Distinctive title**; **Type of composition**.

Gesamtausgabe. *Ger.* The complete works of a composer published in one or more volumes, usually edited from authoritative sources.

Identifying elements. Statements appearing with the title proper of a musical work such as serial number, **opus** or **thematic index** number, key, and date of composition.

Illustrated title page, see **Decorative title page**.

Initial title element. The basis for a uniform title derived from the title proper of a musical work by deleting statements of medium of performance, **identifying elements**, and numerals, adjectives and/or epithets not an integral part of the title.

Label (sound recording). (1) The paper permanently attached to the center of a sound disc or the case of a sound cassette identifying the works recorded and carrying details of publication. (2) The permanently impressed eye-readable information on the top side of a compact digital audio disc. (3) In popular usage, the **label name.** See also **Label name.**

Label name. The trade name, appearing on the **label,** used by a publisher of sound recordings in conjunction with a serial number to identify the particular **release.**

List title page. A title page for printed music that enumerates several musical works offered by the publisher, often with an asterisk or underscore indicating the work contained within.

Medium of performance. The instruments, voices, etc., used in the realization of a musical work.

Music in the popular idiom. Predominantly twentieth-century musical works composed in a style that requires improvisation in performance. Not to be confused with music that is broadly considered to be popular in the sense that it is "well-loved."

Musical presentation statement. The word or phrase appearing on the chief source of information of printed music indicating the physical format of the item (e.g., Score, Partitur, Stimmen, etc.).

Opus number. A number assigned to a musical composition, generally by the publisher and/or composer, to represent the order of composition.

Parts of works, see **Excerpts.**

Popular idiom, Music in the, see **Music in the popular idiom.**

Popular music, see **Music in the popular idiom.**

Popular music folio. A published collection of songs in the popular idiom, often corresponding to one or more sound recordings by the same performer. See also **Music in the popular idiom.**

Program notes, see **Accompanying material.**

Release (Sound recording). Equivalent to the concept of edition, all the copies of a particular performance issued from a single matter recording at one time.

Sleeve (Sound recording). The paper envelope in which a sound disc is issued. See also **Container (Sound recording).**

Thematic index/catalog. A bibliography of the works by a composer, usually arranged chronologically, usually containing reproductions of the themes or the first few measures of each work, and sometimes including a transcription of the autograph score and a complete listing of published editions of each work.

Thematic index number. A number assigned to each musical work of a composer by the compiler of a **thematic index.**

Trade name (Sound recording), see **Label name.**

Type of composition. A form of composition (e.g., sonata), a genre (e.g., bagatelle), or a generic term used by many composers (e.g., piece).

Unit description (Sound recording). A bibliographic record for a sound recording lacking a collective title that includes a transcription of the titles and statements of responsibility for each work performed on the recording.

CONCORDANCE TO RULES/RIs/MCDs

Rule	Source	Page
1.1B3		10
1.1B3(RI)	*MCB* 13:2:3-4	11
1.1F14		9
1.1G2		12
1.4C7		15
1.4C7(RI)	*CSB* 13:3	15
1.4F		16
1.4F6		16
1.5E1(MCD)	*MCB* 12:6:2	26
1.7A3		32
1.7B2(RI)	*CSB* 30:9	28
2.0B1		1
5.0B1		1
5.1B		4
5.1B1		8
5.1B1(RI)	*CSB* 26:10-11	6
5.1B1(RI)	*CSB* 26:10	8
5.1B1(MCD)	*MCB* 16:9:3	6
5.1D1		8
5.1F		9
5.1F1(RI)		10
5.2B2		13
5.2B1(RI)	*CSB* 33:32	14
5.2B2(MCD)	*MCB* 13:6:2	14
5.3		15
5.4		15
5.4F		16
5.5B1		22
5.5B1(MCD)	*MCB* 12:6:2-3	22
5.5B1(MCD)	*MCB* 13:10:2-3	23
5.5B3		24
5.5B3(RI)	*CSB* 33:34	24
5.7B1(MCD)	*MCB* 12:6:3/15:7:3	28
5.7B2		28
5.7B10		29

Compact digital audio discs, xiii, 25-26

Complete works
      for one medium of performance, uniform titles for, 63-65
      of one type of composition, uniform titles for, 63-65
      uniform titles for, 61-66

Composers
      biobibliography, 155-156, 157-160
      complete works of, 62-63
      form of entry for, 39
      selected works of, 63

"Concertante"
      not to be considered part of title in uniform titles, 46

Condensed score(s)
      def. 22

Container (sound recordings)
      def. 161
      notes, 32

Contents notes
      for music, 29-30
      for sound recordings, 33-34

Continuo
      in uniform titles, 49, 50

Contrabassoon
      use in uniform titles, 50

Copy being described notes
      music, 31

Copyright dates
      for music, 16
      for sound recordings, 19

Corporate bodies
      entry under, 39
      names not conveying the idea of, 40

Cover (music), 1
      def. 161

Date of publication, distribution, etc., 16-17, 19-21
      early printed music, 17
      for music, 16-17
      popular music folios, 16-17
      for sound recordings, 19-21

Decorative title page, 1
      def. 161

Key
   in uniform titles, 53-54

Keyboard instrument
   use in uniform titles, 50

Label (sound recordings)
   def. 162

Label name (sound recordings)
   def. 162
   notes, 31-32

Label number (sound recordings)
   notes, 31-32

Language
   in uniform titles, 61
   variants, references for, 83

Language of text notes
   music, 28-29

Library of Congress rule interpretations and music cataloging decisions, xii-xiii, *passim.*

Librettist
   added entries for, sound recordings, 68

Libretto(s)
   entry, choice of, 35-36
   in uniform titles, 57, 64

Lieder
   indication of accompanying medium, xiii
   use in uniform titles, 52

List title page, 1
   def. 162

Literary works
   use in uniform titles, 62-63, 64

Liturgical works
   language in uniform titles for, 61

Liturgical titles
   use as uniform titles, 46

Lizenz Nummer, 16

Mass(es)
   addition of medium of performance to uniform titles for, 48-49

Te deum
        in uniform titles, 46

Text(s)
        use in uniform titles, 58, 64

Thematic indexes
        def. 162
        bibliography, 52-53, 156-160
        numbers, in uniform titles, 52-53
        use for verifying uniform titles, 44

Timpani
        use in uniform titles 50

Title and statement of responsibility area, 4-12

Title added entries, 74-75

Title page substitute
        for music, 1
        for sound recordings, 4

Title proper
        nature of, 4-6
        transcription of, 4-8

Titles
        conflicts in, references, 78-79, 81
        entry of series under, 40
        variant, references for, 76-77, 78-79

Trade name
        of publishers for sound recordings, 19

Translations
        references for, 83
        uniform titles for, 61

Trio(s)
        in uniform titles, 50, 51

Trio sonatas
        use in uniform titles, 47

Types of composition
        def. 162
        names of two or more, in uniform titles, 47

Uniform titles,
        "a due", etc., not to be considered part of title, 46
        for added accompaniments, 59-60
        additions to, for manifestations of works 57-58
        additions to, for modifications of works, 58-61

That Sky, That Rain

That Sky, That Rain

by **Carolyn Otto** • *illustrations by* **Megan Lloyd**

HarperTrophy
A Division of HarperCollinsPublishers

Typography by Andrew Rhodes

Library of Congress Cataloging-in-Publication Data
Otto, Carolyn.
    That sky, that rain / by Carolyn Otto ; illustrations by Megan
Lloyd.
        p.   cm.
    Summary: As a rainstorm approaches, a young girl and her
grandfather take the farm animals into the shelter of the barn and
then watch the rain begin.
    ISBN 0-690-04763-0. — ISBN 0-690-04765-7 (lib. bdg.)
    ISBN 0-06-443290-4 (pbk.)
    [1. Rain and rainfall—Fiction.   2. Farm life—Fiction.]
I. Lloyd, Megan, ill.   II. Title.
PZ7.08794Th 1990   89-36582
[E]—dc20   CIP
                                                              AC

First Harper Trophy edition, 1992.

To Megan, and to my grandparents, Otto and Nicholson, with deep down love.
— CBO

To Carolyn, of course, and to Tom, who saw the rain when there was none.
— MLL

The artist wishes to thank Pete Kutulakis; Cary D'Alo Place; and Dorothy Israel of Birdsong Gordon Setters.

Look at that sky.
We're in for some weather now.

Let's go, Sullivan. Lazybones.
It's going to pour any minute.

I always wanted a beard like that,
like old wire, wire and white paste.
Wouldn't your grandma just die?

Hold out your hands—both hands.
Whoa now. Talk soft now.
See there how her ears come up?

What a racket! What a fuss!
Sullivan, who asked you to sing?

This year I named them after my dinner—
Sweet Corn, Ambrosia, Okra, and Stew.
Stew? says your grandma. Ambrosia!
Next time, she says, I name the pigs.

Come on, Bessie. Come on now.
No sense waiting around for the rain.
Bessie and Bossie, Bossie and Bessie,
those are good names for cows.

Here she comes.

Stand here in the doorway and watch
how rain marks the edges of things—

the overhang of that white awning,

the space beneath the truck.

It's the most commonplace kind of magic,
clouds spilling down before your eyes.

You can open your mouth and drink
sky like a tall glass of water.

Look at that rain!